OpenVZ Essentials

Create and administer virtualized containers on your
server using the robust OpenVZ

Mark Furman

PUBLISHING

BIRMINGHAM - MUMBAI

OpenVZ Essentials

First published: November 2014

Production reference: 1041114

Published by Packt Publishing Ltd.
Livery Place
35 Livery Street
Birmingham B3 2PB, UK.

ISBN 978-1-78216-732-7

www.packtpub.com

Credits

Author
Mark Furman

Reviewers
Emilien Kenler
Unnikrishnan Appukuttan Pillai
Alexei Yuzhakov

Commissioning Editor
Aarthi Kumaraswamy

Acquisition Editor
Meeta Rajani

Content Development Editor
Vaibhav Pawar

Technical Editor
Nikhil Potdukhe

Copy Editors
Roshni Banerjee
Adithi Shetty

Project Coordinator
Kranti Berde

Proofreaders
Ameesha Green
Amy Johnson

Indexers
Mariammal Chettiyar
Monica Ajmera Mehta

Production Coordinators
Manu Joseph
Nilesh R. Mohite
Alwin Roy

Cover Work
Manu Joseph
Nilesh R. Mohite

About the Author

Mark Furman is currently working as a systems engineer for Info-Link Technologies. He has been in the IT field for over 10 years and specializes in Linux and open source technologies. In the past, he has worked as an independent IT contractor providing consulting services for small- to medium-sized businesses and as a Linux administrator for HostGator. He has also been managing his own IT company for several years.

Mark can be reached at m.furman@live.com. He can also be found at www.linkedin.com/in/markfurman and www.twitter.com/mfurman.

I would like to thank my wife, Lynnsey, for being there for me as my support and encouragement while I wrote this book. I would also like to thank my children, Trent, Alissa, Alina, and Kaden, to whom I dedicate this book; my parents, David and Cindy; and my grandparents, Jeanette and Steve, without whom I would not have been the man I am today.

I would like to thank the OpenVZ community for developing, maintaining, and providing support for OpenVZ.

I would like to thank Alexei Yuzhakov for developing OpenVZ Web Panel and reviewing my book.

I would also like to thank the entire Packt Publishing team who made this book possible in the first place. A very special thanks goes out to Meeta Rajani, Vaibhav Pawar, Emilien Kenler, and Nikhil Potdukhe who saw me through the development of this book and provided comments, suggestions, and feedback that helped shape this book.

Finally, I would like to thank you, the readers, for buying this book because without you, there would not have been a reason to write this book in the first place. I hope you enjoy this book as much as I have while writing it for you.

About the Reviewers

Emilien Kenler, after working on small web projects, began to focus on game development in 2008 when he was in high school. Until 2011, he worked for different groups and has specialized in system administration.

In 2011, Emilien founded a company to sell Minecraft servers while he was studying Computer Science Engineering. He created lightweight IaaS based on new technologies, such as Node.js and RabbitMQ. After that, he worked at TaDaweb as a system administrator, building its infrastructure and creating tools to manage deployments and monitoring. In 2014, he began a new adventure at Wizcorp, Tokyo. He graduated in 2014 from The University of Technology of Compiègne.

For Packt Publishing, Emilien has reviewed *Learning Nagios 4*, *Wojciech Kocjan* (http://www.packtpub.com/learning-nagios-4/book), and *MariaDB High Performance*, *Pierre MAVRO* (https://www.packtpub.com/big-data-and-business-intelligence/mariadb-high-performance).

Unnikrishnan Appukuttan Pillai is a Linux system administrator with experience in Linux and open source technologies. He has worked on the latest open source technologies in web hosting, virtualization, and cloud computing. In his 8 years of career, he has worked for leading companies such as Bobcares, IBM, Directi, and KnownHost.

Unnikrishnan has his website at `http://www.mutexes.org/`.

I would like to thank my wife, father, and mother for helping me complete this review.

Alexei Yuzhakov has been working as a development manager of Parallels Plesk Panel. He lives in Novosibirsk, Russia. He likes to drink vodka with bears and code for fun. Software development is not only his job but also his favorite hobby.

www.PacktPub.com

Support files, eBooks, discount offers, and more

You might want to visit www.PacktPub.com for support files and downloads related to your book.

Did you know that Packt offers eBook versions of every book published, with PDF and ePub files available? You can upgrade to the eBook version at www.PacktPub.com and as a print book customer, you are entitled to a discount on the eBook copy. Get in touch with us at service@packtpub.com for more details.

At www.PacktPub.com, you can also read a collection of free technical articles, sign up for a range of free newsletters and receive exclusive discounts and offers on Packt books and eBooks.

http://PacktLib.PacktPub.com

Do you need instant solutions to your IT questions? PacktLib is Packt's online digital book library. Here, you can access, read and search across Packt's entire library of books.

Why subscribe?

- Fully searchable across every book published by Packt
- Copy and paste, print and bookmark content
- On demand and accessible via web browser

Free access for Packt account holders

If you have an account with Packt at www.PacktPub.com, you can use this to access PacktLib today and view nine entirely free books. Simply use your login credentials for immediate access.

Table of Contents

Preface

OpenVZ is one of the most widely used open source container-based virtualization platforms in the world as it allows the user to create multiple Linux-based containers on a single server. This provides the user with the advantage of being able to reduce the number of physical servers on the network, reduce resource and power footprints on the network, and provide a single point of management.

Instead of spending valuable time to take servers down for prolonged periods to add resources such as CPUs, memory, or hard drive space, this can instead be accomplished in minutes using OpenVZ by simply shutting the container down, changing the number of resources that are allocated to the container, and then restarting it.

Taking a practical hands-on approach to learning, the intention of this book is to provide someone with little to no experience of OpenVZ with an opportunity to learn how to install and manage an OpenVZ server from the ground up. By the time you reach the end of this book, you will have a solid understanding of how to administer a server running OpenVZ.

What this book covers

Chapter 1, Installing OpenVZ, discusses virtualization, OpenVZ, and how to install OpenVZ.

Chapter 2, OS Templates and Creating Containers, takes you through OS templates — what they are, and how to download and install them.

Chapter 3, OpenVZ Container Administration, takes you through the concept of a container and its role on an OpenVZ server, how to choose an OS template to use with your container, and how to create a container. It also provides a walkthrough where we create a working container to use with further chapters of this book.

Chapter 4, Server Administration Using OpenVZ, covers all of the essential commands and concepts that the server administrator needs to know to be able to manage the server and containers on the server, including location of important system files, disk quota, CPU management, and memory management.

Chapter 5, Using OpenVZ Web Panel – Part One, takes you through OpenVZ Web Panel. We discuss how OpenVZ Web Panel is related to our OpenVZ server, how to install it, and how to manage your OpenVZ server using OpenVZ Web Panel instead of the Linux command line.

Chapter 6, Using OpenVZ Web Panel – Part Two, picks up from where *Chapter 5, Using OpenVZ Web Panel – Part One*, left off with a discussion on how to configure your OpenVZ Web Panel, and finishes with how to manage your administration tasks using the web panel instead of the Linux command line.

What you need for this book

You will need a spare computer or virtual PC to install Linux OS, and OpenVZ and OpenVZ Web Panel.

Who this book is for

This book is for beginners and intermediate users of OpenVZ who may have some or no experience in using OpenVZ. This book is about how to install and manage the OpenVZ server and containers. It is written from a beginner's perspective from the start.

Conventions

In this book, you will find a number of styles of text that distinguish between different kinds of information. Here are some examples of these styles, and an explanation of their meaning.

Code words in text, database table names, folder names, filenames, file extensions, pathnames, dummy URLs, user input, and Twitter handles are shown as follows: "The next command that we are going to cover is the `vzctl` command."

A block of code is set as follows:

```
ldap:
  enabled: true
  host: "ldap.ldapserver.com"
  login_pattern: "uid=<login>,ou=people,dc=example,dc=com"
```

Any command-line input or output is written as follows:

```
vzctl restart 101
Stopping Container ...
Container was stopped
Container is unmounted
Starting Container...
```

New terms and **important words** are shown in bold. Words that you see on the screen, in menus or dialog boxes for example, appear in the text like this: "The **Remove Template** button allows you to select a template that you want to remove and delete it from the server."

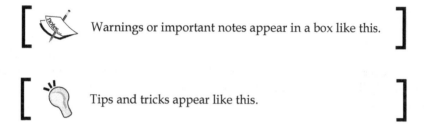

Warnings or important notes appear in a box like this.

Tips and tricks appear like this.

Reader feedback

Feedback from our readers is always welcome. Let us know what you think about this book—what you liked or may have disliked. Reader feedback is important for us to develop titles that you really get the most out of.

To send us general feedback, simply send an e-mail to `feedback@packtpub.com`, and mention the book title via the subject of your message.

If there is a topic that you have expertise in and you are interested in either writing or contributing to a book, see our author guide on `www.packtpub.com/authors`.

Customer support

Now that you are the proud owner of a Packt book, we have a number of things to help you to get the most from your purchase.

Errata

Although we have taken every care to ensure the accuracy of our content, mistakes do happen. If you find a mistake in one of our books—maybe a mistake in the text or the code—we would be grateful if you would report this to us. By doing so, you can save other readers from frustration and help us improve subsequent versions of this book. If you find any errata, please report them by visiting `http://www.packtpub.com/submit-errata`, selecting your book, clicking on the **errata submission form** link, and entering the details of your errata. Once your errata are verified, your submission will be accepted and the errata will be uploaded on our website, or added to any list of existing errata, under the Errata section of that title. Any existing errata can be viewed by selecting your title from `http://www.packtpub.com/support`.

Piracy

Piracy of copyright material on the Internet is an ongoing problem across all media. At Packt, we take the protection of our copyright and licenses very seriously. If you come across any illegal copies of our works, in any form, on the Internet, please provide us with the location address or website name immediately so that we can pursue a remedy.

Please contact us at `copyright@packtpub.com` with a link to the suspected pirated material.

We appreciate your help in protecting our authors, and our ability to bring you valuable content.

Questions

You can contact us at `questions@packtpub.com` if you are having a problem with any aspect of the book, and we will do our best to address it.

1
Installing OpenVZ

In this chapter, we are going to explain what OpenVZ is and the system requirements we need to install OpenVZ on our system. Then we are going to walk through configuring yum to use the OpenVZ repo and install the vzkernel.

Finally, we are going to talk about installing additional packages to help manage containers on the node—vzctl to create, configure, and remove containers and vzquota to manage quotas.

What is OS-level virtualization?

OS-level virtualization is a type of virtualization that is kernel-based. It depends on a host OS to manage, create, and configure containers on the host server through a specialized kernel.

Another type of virtualization is bare bones virtualization; this type of virtualization differs from the OS-level virtualization by providing a small OS that is booted instead of a host OS such as Windows or Linux. This type of virtualization is used to reduce the resource overhead on the host OS.

What is OpenVZ?

OpenVZ is a OS-level virtualization software that allows you to run isolated, secured containers that use a modified version of the Linux kernel to split the physical server to allow you to run multiple isolated containers, sometimes also called virtual private servers, that act as their own independent servers and have their own properties that are:

- Root account
- Users

- Filesystem and quotas
- Processes
- Memory limits
- CPU quotas
- Network configuration

Each of the containers shares the same hardware and resources from a single physical server called a node.

The operating systems on the server cannot be mixed; they must run the same operating system as the physical server. Since you are using Linux for OpenVZ, you can only install Linux containers, although you can use different distributions of Linux for each of your containers.

System requirements

For this book, you are going to use CentOS 6.5 as the distribution OS in all the examples. You can also follow RHEL6.5, Scientific Linux, or Debian 7 along with this book. At the time of this writing, the OpenVZ kernel version that is available is vzkernel 2.6.32 and will be the OpenVZ kernel that is used throughout the rest of this book.

For hardware specifications, the following are recommended:

- IBM PC compatible computer
- Intel Core i7, Xeon E7, and AMD Opteron
- A minimum of 128 MB of RAM; 2 GB or more is recommended
- A hard drive with at least 80 GB of space
- A 10/100/1000 network card

For network specifications, the following are recommended:

- A local area network for the server
- A valid Internet connection
- A valid IP address for the server
- A valid IP address for each container

Please note that the previously listed requirements are recommended to get you started with learning how to use OpenVZ. On a live server, you will want to increase the RAM and CPU as the number of your containers grows on the server. It is not unusual to see a server with three to four CPUs with two or more cores at 3.4 GHz per core and 90 GB of RAM.

The disk partition scheme

You will create a / partition for Centos 6.5 and a swap partition to manage the virtual memory on the server and a /vz partition to store the containers that are created on the server.

When installing your Linux distribution, you will want to configure your disk partition scheme to the following:

Partition	Size
/	4-12 GB
Swap	Twice the amount of RAM
/vz	Rest of the space on the drive

The yum configuration

First, we will start by adding the OpenVZ repo to the repos.d directory under /etc/yum/; you can do this by running the following command:

```
wget -P /etc/yum.repos.d/ http://ftp.openvz.org/openvz.repo
```

In the previous example, we use the wget command to download the openvz.repo file from ftp.openvz.org to install openvz.repo on your server.

Then, import the OpenVZ GPG key used to sign the packages by running the following command:

```
rpm --import http://ftp.openvz.org/RPM-GPG-Key-OpenVZ
```

In the previous example, we use the rpm command to import the GPG key for openvz.repo to validate the package as a signed package.

Installing vzkernel

Vzkernel is the core of OpenVZ; it is essentially a modified version of the Linux kernel that allows you to run containers on your server.

To install vzkernel, you will want to run the following command:

```
yum install vzkernel
```

In the previous example, we use the `yum` command with the `install` option to install `vzkernel` on our server.

Installing vzctl and vzquota

In this section, we are going to go over the additional tools that are needed to install the vzkernel. The tools are as follows:

- **vzctl**: This is an OpenVZ utility tool that allows you to directly interface with the containers. You can use this utility to start, stop, suspend, destroy, and create containers. We will go over this utility and it's usage in more detail in a future chapter.

- **vzquota**: This is an OpenVZ utility that allows you to configure disk quotas on your server. You can use this utility to initialize, turn quotas on, turn quotas off, set limits, and show quota stats. We will go over this utility and it's usage in more detail in a following chapter.

To install the utilities, you will need to run the following command:

```
yum install vzctl vzquota
```

In the previous example, we use the `yum` command to install the packages for `vzctl`, `vzquota`, and `ploop` on the server.

Restarting the server

The last step you need to perform is rebooting your server by executing the following command. When the server comes back up, your OpenVZ installation will be complete and you will have a running OpenVZ server.

```
shutdown -r now
```

Summary

In this chapter, we discussed what OpenVZ is and walked through the system requirements to install OpenVZ, including hardware and networking requirements. Finally, we walked through the steps needed to install OpenVZ—configuring yum, and installing the vzkernel and additional utilities: vzctl and vzquota.

In the next chapter, you are going to learn how to download and use OS templates to create containers on the server as well as how to create a container and set up the hostname, IP address, and DNS for it.

2
OS Templates and Creating Containers

In the previous chapter, we went over how to set up and install OpenVZ. In this chapter, we are going to walk through the download of OS templates that we will be using as default templates for our containers. Then, we will discuss how to create the container itself and add the default configurations necessary to make the container operational.

These are the topics that we are going to cover in this chapter:

- What are OS templates?
- How to download templates to your server?
- How to properly choose a container ID?
- How to create a container?
- How to set the hostname, IP address, and DNS server for the container?

Getting started with OS templates

OS templates are packed container files of a Linux distribution that we can use to quickly install a new container on our node. We can use multiple distributions of Linux on the OpenVZ node. We are not confined to use the same distribution that is installed on the server itself.

You cannot, however, use Windows templates because OpenVZ is an OS-level virtualization technology. The packaged files inside the template files contain everything that is needed to run the container, including boot files, libraries, and system utilities.

Downloading OS templates

Two ways to download OS templates are explained in this section—one method is by using `vztmpl-dl` and the other method is a manual method.

Using vztmpl-dl to download OS templates

OpenVZ comes with a tool named `vztmpl-dl` that can help you download OS templates easily and effectively. You will use two options with `vztmpl-dl`, which are explained as follows:

- `vztmpl-dl --list-remote`: This command will provide a list of available OS templates that you are able to download.

- `vztmpl-dl [template file]`: This command will allow you to download the OS template that you picked using the `--list-remote` option. For example, you can use this command to download an OS template for CentOS 6.5 64-bit with the following command:

  `vztmpl-dl centos-6-x86_64`

  In the previous example, you used the `vztmpl-dl` command to download an OS template for CentOS 6.5.

Manually downloading OS templates

The core template files are maintained by OpenVZ and are available for download at `http://download.openvz.org/template/precreated`. There are also templates that are maintained by the OpenVZ community. These templates are available at `http://download.openvz.org/template/precreated/contrib/`. The default directory where you want to save the template is in the `cache` directory under `/vz/template/` of your server.

For this book, we are going to use the `centos-6-x86.tar.gz` template file, but feel free to download and install any one of the listed distributions that you like. You can see that besides CentOS, you can also choose Debian, Fedora, Scientific Linux, SUSE, and Ubuntu as your installation.

Type the following commands to download the CentOS 6 template:

```
cd /vz/template/cache
wget    "http://download.openvz.org/template/precreated/centos-6-x86.tar.
gz"
```

In the previous example, you first changed your directory to /vz/template/cache and then used wget to download the CentOS 6 template in the same directory.

Selecting a container ID

After downloading the OS template that we are going to use to create our first container, the next step is to choose a **container ID** (**CTID**). A container ID is a numeric ID that is assigned to the container when it is created. When choosing a container ID, there are a few things that you should remember:

- Every container ID needs to be unique. You cannot use the same ID more than once on the same container.

- ID 0 is the container ID for your server. You will not be able to use 0 for your container ID.

- The best practice is to start your naming scheme after 101. This is because the range 0-100 is reserved for OpenVZ internal purposes.

- For the remaining examples in the book, we are going to use the container ID of 101 to configure and create containers on the server.

Selecting an OS template

After figuring out what CTID you would like to use for your container, the next step is to choose the OS template that you want to use for your container. In the *Downloading OS templates* section, we chose to use the OS template for CentOS 6 for our example. You can list the available templates by using ls on the /vz/template/cache directory.

Creating a container

After selecting which OS template you are going to use, you need to create a container in the next step. To create the container, you will need to use the `vzctl create` command. In order to use the `vzctl create` command, you have to supply the command with arguments for both the container ID that you chose (101) and also the OS template that you chose (`centos-6-x86.tar.gz`). You will also use the basic configuration file for the installation (`ve-basic.conf-sample`). We will talk more about this file shortly.

To create the VPS container, perform the following steps:

1. Firstly, execute the following command:

   ```
   vzctl create 101 --ostemplate centos-6-x86 --config basic
   ```

   This will create a container on the server. To verify that the container has been created, you can use the `vzlist` command. The `vzlist` command will display all the containers that are created on the server.

2. To view the list of containers on the server, execute the following command:

   ```
   vzlist -a
   ```

In the previous example, we used `vzlist` with an a flag that allows us to list all the containers that are either stopped or are running on the server. You will see container `101` listed as a newly created container.

The output will look like this:

```
CTID    NPROC STATUS     IP_ADDR          HOSTNAME
 101       17 stopped    -                -
```

Container configuration

The final steps that we need to take are to configure our new container to start up on boot. So, when we reset the server, the containers will automatically boot. We also need to configure the network settings for the container: hostname, IP address, and name server information. Finally, we will need to provide the container with a root password.

To configure these settings, we will use the `vzctl set` command. This command will allow you to add, remove, and modify configuration settings inside the container's conf file, which is located at `/etc/vz/conf/` and named `101.conf`.

Configuring a container to start on boot

We will use `vzctl set` to modify the `onboot` option inside the container's `config` file which will be set to `yes` using the `--onboot` flag. This will allow the container to automatically boot when the node is restarted. We will also use the `--save` flag to tell the command to save the changes to the configuration file.

To set the `onboot` option to `yes`, use the following command:

```
vzctl set 101 --onboot yes --save
```

In the previous example, we used `vzctl` with the `set` option on our container that was created (`101`) to change the container configuration setting for `onboot` from `no` to `yes`, which allows us to boot the container when the server starts up instead of us starting the container manually and then saving the settings to `/etc/vz/conf/101/conf`.

Setting the hostname

Now, we will configure the network settings for the container. The first setting we are going to look at is configuring the hostname. You can call your hostname whatever you like, as long as you own the domain. For the purpose of this book, I will be using the name `gotham.mydomain.com`.

To configure the hostname, execute the following command:

```
vzctl set 101 --hostname gotham.mydomain.com --save
```

In the previous example, we used `vzctl` with the `set` option on the container that was created (`101`) to change the configuration setting for the hostname to `gotham. mydomain.com` and then saved the settings to `/etc/vz/conf/101.conf`.

Setting an IP address

The next part of the network configuration is setting the IP address for the container. We will want to use an IP address that we have delegated for this server. For the purpose of this book, I have set up a network IP range of `192.168.1.1` to `192.168.1.255`. I allocated two IP addresses from this range, one for the node itself (`192.168.1.100`) and one for the container (`192.168.1.101`).

To configure the IP address, execute the following command:

```
vzctl set 101 --ipadd 192.168.1.101 --save
```

In the previous example, we used `vzctl` with the `set` option on the container that was created (`101`) to change the configuration setting for the IP address of your container to `192.168.1.101` and then saved the settings to `/etc/vz/conf/101.conf`.

Setting a name server

The final part of setting up the network configuration settings is configuring the DNS settings for the container. You can set up your own name servers, but this is beyond the scope of this book. To make things easy, we are going to use the Google public DNS settings (`8.8.8.8`) for our name server.

To configure the DNS server, execute the following command:

```
vzctl set 101 --nameserver 8.8.8.8 --save
```

In the previous example, we used `vzctl` with the `set` option on the container that was created (`101`) to change the configuration setting for `nameserver` to point to the Google DNS address of `8.8.8.8` and then saved the settings to `/etc/vz/conf/101.conf`.

Setting the root password

The final step that we need to perform to finish the configuration of our VPS container is to set the root password for the container.

The reason for doing this is that the root account is disabled by default when the container is created, so we have to enable the account to grant access to the root account through `ssh`.

For the following example, you will be using the user `root` and the password `changeme`. I strongly suggest that you set your password to a more secure one. To enable the account and change the password, execute the following command:

```
vzctl set 101 --userpasswd root:changeme
```

In the previous example, we used `vzctl` with the `set` option on the container that was previously created (container `101`) to change the password for the root user by using the `--userpasswd` flag to set the password as `changeme`.

VE configuration files

VE configuration files are files that are located in /etc/vz/conf on the server.
In /etc/vz/conf, you will see a configuration file created for every container on the
server, sample configuration files such as ve-basic.conf-sample (which previously
was used to create the container) and ve-skeleton-conf.sample (which is a default
conf file that contains default settings).

Summary

In this chapter, we learned how to download an OS template that we can use to
quickly create a VPS container that is using CentOS, Fedora, Scientific Linux, SUSE,
Debian, or Ubuntu. We also learned how to use the vzctl create command to
create a VPS container on the node.

Finally, we learned about the vzlist command that can list the VPS containers
that are created on the server and also learned about the vzctl command that we
use to change settings from the containers configuration file, including starting
the container on node boot; how to set the hostname, IP address, name server;
and changing the root password.

In the next chapter, we will learn how to start, stop, suspend, and resume containers.
We will also learn how to destroy, mount, and unmount containers; set file and disk
quotas for containers; and create snapshots of containers in order to back up, restore,
or migrate a container to another server.

3
OpenVZ Container Administration

In the previous chapter, we learned how to create a container. In this chapter, we will go over the various aspects of OpenVZ administration. Some of the things we are going to go over in this chapter are as follows:

- Listing the containers that are running on the server
- Starting, stopping, suspending, and resuming containers
- Destroying, mounting, and unmounting containers
- Setting quota on and off
- Creating snapshots of the containers in order to back up and restore the container to another server

Using vzlist

The `vzlist` command is used to list the containers on a node. When you run `vzlist` on its own without any options, it will only list the containers that are currently running on the system:

```
vzlist
```

In the previous example, we used the `vzlist` command to list the containers that are currently running on the server.

Listing all the containers on the server

If you want to list all the containers on the server instead of just the containers that are currently running on the server, you will need to add -a after vzlist. This will tell vzlist to include all of the containers that are created on the node inside its output:

```
vzlist -a
```

In the previous example, we used the vzlist command with an -a flag to tell vzctl that we want to list all of the containers that have been created on the server.

The vzctl command

The next command that we are going to cover is the vzctl command. This is the primary command that you are going to use when you want to perform tasks with the containers on the node. The initial functions of the vzctl command that we will go over are how to start, stop, and restart the container.

Starting a container

We use vzctl to start a container on the node. To start a container, run the following command:

```
vzctl start 101
```

```
Starting Container ...
Setup slm memory limit
Setup slm subgroup (default)
Setting devperms 20002 dev 0x7d00
Adding IP address(es) to pool:
Adding IP address(es): 192.168.2.101
Hostname for Container set: gotham.example.com
Container start in progress...
```

In the previous example, we used the vzctl command with the start option to start the container 101.

Stopping a container

To stop a container, run the following command:

```
vzctl stop 101
Stopping container ...
```

```
Container was stopped
Container is unmounted
```

In the previous example, we used the vzctl command with the stop option to stop the container 101.

Restarting a container

To restart a container, run the following command:

```
vzctl restart 101
Stopping Container ...
Container was stopped
Container is unmounted
Starting Container...
```

In the previous example, we used the vzctl command with the restart option to restart the container 101.

Using vzctl to suspend and resume a container

The following set of commands will use vzctl to suspend and resume a container. When you use vzctl to suspend a container, it creates a save point of the container to a dump file. You can then use vzctl to resume the container to the saved point it was in before the container was suspended.

Suspending a container

To suspend a container, run the following command:

```
vzctl suspend 101
```

In the previous example, we used the vzctl command with the suspend option to suspend the container 101.

Resuming a container

To resume a container, run the following command:

```
vzctl resume 101
```

In the previous example, we used the `vzctl` command with the `resume` option to resume operations on the container `101`.

 In order to get resume or suspend to work, you may need to enable several kernel modules by running the following:

```
modprobe vzcpt
modprobe vzrst
```

Destroying a container

You can destroy a container that you created by using the `destroy` argument with `vzctl`. This will remove all the files including the configuration file and the directories created by the container. In order to destroy a container, you must first stop the container from running.

To destroy a container, run the following command:

```
vzctl destroy 101
Destroying container private area: /vz/private/101
```

Container private area was destroyed.

In the previous example, we used the `vzctl` command with the `destroy` option to destroy the container `101`.

Using vzctl to mount and unmount a container

You are able to mount and unmount a container's private area located at `/vz/root/ctid`, which provides the container with root filesystem that exists on the server. Mounting and unmounting containers come in handy when you have trouble accessing the filesystem for your container.

Mounting a container

To mount a container, run the following command:

```
vzctl mount  101
```

In the previous example, we used the `vzctl` command with the `mount` option to mount the private area for the container `101`.

Unmounting a container

To unmount a container, run the following command:

```
vzctl umount 101
```

In the previous example, we used the `vzctl` command with the `umount` option to unmount the private area for the container `101`

Disk quotas

Disk quotas allow you to define special limits for your container, including the size of the filesystem or the number of inodes that are available for use.

Setting quotaon and quotaoff for a container

You can manually start and stop the containers disk quota by using the `quotaon` and `quotaoff` arguments with `vzctl`.

Turning on disk quota for a container

To turn on disk quota for a container, run the following command:

```
vzctl quotaon 101
```

In the previous example, we used the `vzctl` command with the `quotaon` option to turn disk quota on for the container `101`.

Turning off disk quota for a container

To turn off disk quota for a container, run the following command:

```
vzctl quotaoff 101
```

In the previous example, we used the `vzctl` command with the `quotaoff` option to turn off disk quota for the container `101`.

Setting disk quotas with vzctl set

You are able to set the disk quotas for your containers on your server using the `vzctl set` command. With this command, you can set the disk space, disk inodes, and the quota time.

To set the disk space for container `101` to 2 GB, use the following command:

```
vzctl set 101 --diskspace 2000000:2200000 --save
```

In the previous example, we used the `vzctl set` command to set the disk space quota to 2 GB with a 2.2 GB barrier. The two values that are separated with a `:` symbol and are the soft limit and the hard limit. The soft limit in the example is `2000000` and the hard limit is `2200000`. The soft limit can be exceeded up to the value of the hard limit. The hard limit should never exceed its value. OpenVZ defines soft limits as barriers and hard limits as limits. We will discuss these values further in *Chapter 4, Server Administration Using OpenVZ*.

To set the `inode` disk for container `101` to 1 million inodes, use the following command:

```
vzctl set 101 --diskinodes 1000000:1100000 --save
```

In the previous example, we used the `vzctl set` command to set the disk inode limits to a soft limit or barrier of 1 million inodes and a hard limit or limit or 1.1 million inodes.

To set the quota time or the period of time in seconds that the container is allowed to exceed the soft limit values of disk quota and inode quota, use the following command:

```
vzctl set 101 --quotatime 900 --save
```

In the previous example, we used the `vzctl` command to set the quota time to 900 seconds or 15 minutes. This means that once the container soft limit is broken, you will be able to exceed the quota to the value of the hard limit for 15 minutes before the container reports that the value is over quota.

Further use of vzctl set

The `vzctl set` command allows you to make modifications to the container's config file without the need to manually edit the file. We are going to go over a few of the options that are essential to administer the node.

--onboot

The --onboot flag allows you to set whether or not the container will be booted when the node is booted.

To set the onboot option, use the following command:

```
vzctl set  101 --onboot
```

In the previous example, we used the vzctl command with the set option and the --onboot flag to enable the container to boot automatically when the server is rebooted, and then saved to the container configuration file.

--bootorder

The --bootorder flag allows you to change the boot order priority of the container. The higher the value given, the sooner the container will start when the node is booted.

To set the bootorder option, use the following command:

```
vzctl set  101 --bootorder  9 --save
```

In the previous example, we used the vzctl command with the set option and the bootorder flag to tell that we would like to change the priority of the order that the container is booted in, and then we save the option to the container's configuration file.

--userpasswd

The --userpasswd flag allows you to change a user's password that belongs to the container. If the user does not exist, then the user will be created.

To set the userpasswd option, use the following command:

```
vzctl set 101 --userpasswd admin:changeme
```

In the previous example, we used the vzctl command with the set option and the --userpasswd flag and change the password for the admin user to the password changeme.

--name

The --name flag allows you to give the container a name that when assigned, can be used in place of the CTID value when using vzctl. This allows for an easier way to memorize your containers. Instead of focusing on the container ID, you will just need to remember the container name to access the container.

To set the name option, use the following command:

```
vzctl set 101 --name gotham --save
```

In the previous example, we used the vzctl command with the set option to set our container 101 to use the name gotham and then save the changes to containers configuration file.

--description

The --description flag allows you to add a description for the container to give an idea of what the container is for.

To use the description option, use the following command:

```
vzctl set 101 --description  "Web Development Test Server" --save
```

In the previous example, we used the vzctl command with the set option and the --description flag to add a description of the container "Web Development Test Server".

--ipadd

The --ipadd flag allows you to add an IP address to the specified container.

To set the ipadd option, use the following command:

```
vzctl set 101 --ipadd 192.168.2.103 --save
```

In the previous example, we used the vzctl command with the set option and the -ipadd flag to add the IP address 192.168.2.103 to container 101 and then save the changes to the containers configuration file.

--ipdel

The --ipdel flag allows you to remove an IP address from the specified container.

To use the ipdel option, use the following command:

```
vzctl set 101 --ipdel 192.168.2.103 --save
```

In the previous example, we used the `vzctl` command with the `set` option and the `--ipdel` flag to remove the IP address `192.168.2.193` from the container `101` and then save the changes to the containers configuration file.

--hostname

The `--hostname` flag allows you to set or change the hostname for your container.

To use the `hostname` option, use the following command:

```
vzctl set 101 --hostname gotham.example.com --save
```

In the previous example, we used the `vzctl` command with the `set` option and the `--hostname` flag to change the hostname of the container to `gotham.example.com`.

--disable

The `--disable` flag allows you to disable a containers startup. When this option is in place, you will not be able to start the container until this option is removed.

To use the `disable` option, use the following command:

```
vzctl set 101 --disable
```

In the preceding example, we used the `vzctl` command with the `set` option and the `--disable` flag to prevent the container `101` from starting and then save the changes to the container's configuration file.

--ram

The `--ram` flag allows you to set the value for the physical page limit of the container and helps to regulate the amount of memory that is available to the container.

To use the `ram` option, use the following command:

```
vzctl set 101 --ram 2G --save
```

In the previous example, we set the physical page limit to 2 GB using the `--ram` flag.

--swap

The `--swap` flag allows you to set the value of the amount of swap memory that is available to the container.

To use the swap option, use the following command:

```
vzctl set 101 --swap 1G --save
```

In the preceding example, we set the swap memory limit for the container to 1 GB using the --swap flag.

Summary

In this chapter, we learned to administer the containers that are created on the node by using the vzctl command, and the vzlist command to list containers on the server. The vzctl command has a broad range of flags that can be given to it to allow you to perform many actions to a container.

It allows you to start, stop, and restart, create, and destroy a container. You can also suspend and unsuspend the current state of the container, mount and unmount a container, issue changes to the container's config file by using vzctl set.

In the next chapter, we will learn how to manage resources on the node. Some of the things that we will go over are important system files, how to manage CPU and RAM resource usage, how to utilize /proc/user/beancounters, and how to apply server-wide quotas and logfiles.

4
Server Administration Using OpenVZ

In this chapter, we are going to change the focus from administering the container to briefly discussing administering tasks on the server.

We are going to cover the following topics:

- Important system files
- CPU management
- Memory management
- Important logfiles

Important system files

In this section, we are going to go over the important system files that you will interact with administering OpenVZ on your server included in the following directories:

- `/etc/vz`
- `/vz`
- `/proc/user_beancounter`

Understanding the /etc/vz directory

The /etc/vz directory is the main configuration directory for OpenVZ that contains several important files in it, such as dists, osrelease.conf, and vz.conf. You will also see a symlink named conf that links to the /sysconfig/vz-scripts directory.

- dists: This file contains information about container actions that need to be handled in a specific way as per the distribution that the container is using. A good example of this is if you are using an Ubuntu distribution and you want to change the hostname, the hostname change would be written to /etc/hostname.

- osrelease.conf: This file provides a list to vzctl at the startup of the container that checks the distribution of the container and the required kernel version.

- vz.conf: This file is the global configuration file for OpenVZ. Any changes that are made to this file are changed server wide inside the file. You will find files for global settings such as the location of the lock directory (default is /vz/lock), turning system logging on and off, setting the location of the logfile (default is /var/log/vzctl.log), and the log level (default is 0) that defines how much information is written to the logfile. The higher the number you choose, the more information is written. You will also find information for network parameters, defaults for vzcreate, and defaults for containers.

Understanding the /vz directory

The /vz directory is where the actual files for the containers reside for your OpenVZ server. The following is information about the directories located inside /vz:

- /vz/private: The directory where the files of your container are located
- vz/template/cache: The directory where the OS templates are located
- /vz/lock: The directory where the vz lock file is stored
- /vz/dump: The directory where the output after running vzdump is stored
- /vz/root: The directory where the container mount points are located

Understanding the /proc/user_beancounters file

The `/proc/user_beancounters` file is a resource tool that allows us to see the set of limits that are given for each container to prevent them from using all the resources on the server.

The following is an example output of `/proc/user_beancounters`:

```
[root@gotham ~]# cat /proc/user_beancounters
Version: 2.5
       uid  resource              held        maxheld          barrier            limit     failcnt
       101: kmemsize           3941661        4870144        121634816        134217728           0
            lockedpages              0              0            32768            32768           0
            privvmpages          11397          13513  9223372036854775807  9223372036854775807           0
            shmpages               129            129  9223372036854775807  9223372036854775807           0
            dummy                    0              0                0                0           0
            numproc                 17             27  9223372036854775807  9223372036854775807           0
            physpages             8790           9645                0            65536           0
            vmguarpages              0              0                0  9223372036854775807           0
            oomguarpages          1851           1962                0  9223372036854775807           0
            numtcpsock               4              4  9223372036854775807  9223372036854775807           0
            numflock                 4              5  9223372036854775807  9223372036854775807           0
            numpty                   0              1  9223372036854775807  9223372036854775807           0
            numsiginfo               0             12  9223372036854775807  9223372036854775807           0
            tcpsndbuf            69760          69760  9223372036854775807  9223372036854775807           0
            tcprcvbuf            65536          65536  9223372036854775807  9223372036854775807           0
            othersockbuf          4624          31576  9223372036854775807  9223372036854775807           0
            dgramrcvbuf              0              0  9223372036854775807  9223372036854775807           0
            numothersock            24             30  9223372036854775807  9223372036854775807           0
            dcachesize         1126990        1138826  9223372036854775807  9223372036854775807           0
            numfile                295            350  9223372036854775807  9223372036854775807           0
            dummy                    0              0                0                0           0
            dummy                    0              0                0                0           0
            dummy                    0              0                0                0           0
            numiptent               14             20  9223372036854775807  9223372036854775807           0
        0:  kmemsize          20523246       20750336  9223372036854775807  9223372036854775807           0
            lockedpages              0           3640  9223372036854775807  9223372036854775807           0
            privvmpages          50809          68341  9223372036854775807  9223372036854775807           0
            shmpages               690            706  9223372036854775807  9223372036854775807           0
            dummy                    0              0  9223372036854775807  9223372036854775807           0
            numproc                 89            139  9223372036854775807  9223372036854775807           0
            physpages            76416          76905  9223372036854775807  9223372036854775807           0
            vmguarpages              0              0  9223372036854775807  9223372036854775807           0
            oomguarpages         30533          41044  9223372036854775807  9223372036854775807           0
            numtcpsock              67            106  9223372036854775807  9223372036854775807           0
            numflock                 2              7  9223372036854775807  9223372036854775807           0
            numpty                   1              1  9223372036854775807  9223372036854775807           0
            numsiginfo               1            132  9223372036854775807  9223372036854775807           0
            tcpsndbuf          1168480        1848640  9223372036854775807  9223372036854775807           0
            tcprcvbuf          1108232        1820736  9223372036854775807  9223372036854775807           0
            othersockbuf        120224         164928  9223372036854775807  9223372036854775807           0
            dgramrcvbuf              0           1288  9223372036854775807  9223372036854775807           0
            numothersock           100            104  9223372036854775807  9223372036854775807           0
            dcachesize        15116695       15131264  9223372036854775807  9223372036854775807           0
            numfile                595            665  9223372036854775807  9223372036854775807           0
            dummy                    0              0  9223372036854775807  9223372036854775807           0
            dummy                    0              0  9223372036854775807  9223372036854775807           0
            dummy                    0              0  9223372036854775807  9223372036854775807           0
            numiptent               26             32  9223372036854775807  9223372036854775807           0
```

The following are some of the fields that you will see listed in the `/proc/user_beancounters` file:

- `uid`: This is the numeric identifier of the container.

- `resource`: This is a list of the resources that you currently want to find information for. I will discuss resources in more detail in the *Resources* section of this chapter.

- `held`: The current usage value of a resource.

- `maxheld`: The total amount of resource usage of a container based on the container's total lifetime.

- `barrier`: The control resources that are variable to the resource whose value should not exceed the value for limit.

- `limit`: The control resources that are variable and are set as the maximum value. Normally, this is set higher than the barrier limit.

Resources

Resources are the physical limits that can be set and controlled for the server. They can also be set on a per-container basis.

- `kmemsize`: Determines how much memory the kernel is allowed to use for tracking processes

- `lockedpages`: The process pages that cannot be swapped out of memory

- `privmpages`: Allows you to control the amount of memory that is allocated by applications

- `shmpages`: This is the total amount of shared memory that is allocated for the server

- `dummy`: The reservation marker or place holder for future resource allocation use

- `numproc`: The total number of processes that a container can spawn on the server

- `physpages`: The total number of pages that are being used by resources inside a container

- `vmguarpages`: The guaranteed amount of VM paging for each container
- `oomguarpages`: The amount of memory that is being used by the processes of a container
- `numtcpsock`: The total number of TCP sockets that are available for a server
- `numflock`: The number of file locks that are allowed for each container
- `numpty`: The number of shell sessions that are allowed at once on a server
- `numsigninfo`: The number of signinfo structures that are allowed at one time on a server
- `tcpsndbuf`: Sets the total size of packet buffers used to send data over a TCP connection on the server and each individual container
- `tcprcvbuf`: Sets the packet buffers that are used to temporarily store the data that is coming from TCP network connections on the server and each individual container
- `othersockbuf`: This is the total size domain socket buffers that UDP and other datagram protocols use to send packet buffers
- `dgramrcvbuf`: The total size of packet buffers that are used to temporarily store incoming packets of UDP and other datagram protocols
- `numothersock`: This is the maximum number of UDP sockets that are available
- `dcachesize`: This is the total size of the dentry and inode structures that are locked into physical memory on the server
- `numfile`: This is the total number of open files on the server
- `numipent`: This is the total number of Netfilter entries that are currently on the server

Managing and configuring the CPU

In this section, we are going to cover CPU management, including how to manage CPU share and configuring the number of CPUs inside more than one container.

CPU share

You can use the OpenVZ CPU resource utilities to allot to any container a guarantee of the amount of CPU time it receives.

vzcpucheck

We use the `vzcpucheck` command to check the current hardware node CPU utilization using the following command:

vzcpucheck

```
[root@gotham ~]# vzcpucheck
Current CPU utilization: 2501
Power of the node: 159625
[root@gotham ~]# _
```

In the previous example, we can see that when we run `vzcpucheck`, **Current CPU utilization** is **2501** (this is the total number of CPU units consumed by the running container and processes on the server) and **Power of the node** is **159625** (which is the total CPU processing power).

In this example, we used the `vzcpucheck` command to show our changes to the current CPU utilization for the container `101`.

Setting up a container to use a set amount of CPU units

To set the container to use a set amount of CPU time, we use the following `vzctl` command:

vzctl set 101 --cpuunits 1500 --cpulimit 4 --save

```
[root@gotham ~]# vzctl set 101 --cpuunits 1500 --cpulimit 4 --save
Setting CPU limit: 4
Setting CPU units: 1500
Saved parameters for CT 101
[root@gotham ~]# $$$_
```

In this example, we used the `vzctl` command with the `set` option and the `cpuunits` flag with the value of `1500` to set the minimum guaranteed share of CPU time container `101` will receive. Then, we used the `-cpulimit` flag with the value of `4` to indicate the CPU time in percentage that container 101 is not allowed to exceed. Finally, we used the `-save` flag to save our settings.

Configuring the number of CPUs used by a container

You can configure the number of CPUs used by a container if your server has more than one processor installed. The advantage of this is that it will either allow you to prevent a container from using the full amount of CPU resources on the server, or it will allow you to dedicate more CPU resource usage to a container.

To set a container to use a set amount of CPUs, run the following command:

```
vzctl set 101 --cpus 2 --save
```

In the previous example, we used the `vzctl` command with the `set` option and the `-cpus` flag to set the maximum CPU resource value on container 101 to 2 CPUs.

To check that the changes to the CPU limit have been made, you can run `cat /proc/cpuinfo | grep "processor"` from inside your container. Run the `cat /proc/cpuinfo | grep "processor"` command as shown in the following screenshot:

```
[root@Gotham /]# cat /proc/cpuinfo |grep "processor"
processor       : 0
processor       : 1
[root@Gotham /]# _
```

In the previous example, we used `cat /proc/cpuinfo | grep "processor"` to display information about the CPU usage inside container 101. This shows us that we have two processors that are assigned to the container — processor `0` and processor `1`, and the changes we made with `vzctl` to set our container to use two processors are complete.

Memory management

One of the features of OpenVZ is that it allows you to manage the memory allocation to the containers on a very fine-tuned level and allows you to fully control memory resources on the node.

vzmemcheck

You can use `vzmemcheck` to check the amount of memory that is currently being used by the server and also by each individual container. Using `vzmemcheck` on its own will give you the memory usage that is currently being used by the entire server. This is shown in the following screenshot:

```
[root@gotham ~]# vzmemcheck
Output values in %
 LowMem  LowMem      RAM MemSwap MemSwap    Alloc    Alloc   Alloc
  util   commit     util    util  commit     util   commit   limit
  1.18 8868740482688.47    4.02    0.40 1169770694531.77     1.64 1169770694531.77 1199014961890702.25
```

In the previous example, we used the `vzmemcheck` command with no options or flags to display the current memory that is being used by the server.

LowMem

LowMem is the part of memory that is directly available by the OS kernel.

MemSwap

MemSwap is a joining of both the physical memory and swap on the server. This determines the total amount of memory that is available for applications.

Allocated

Allocated memory shows the total amount of memory that is currently allocated for use for future processes on the server.

vzmemcheck with the -v flag

You can also use `vzmemcheck` with the `-v` flag to check the amount of memory that is currently being used per container. This allows you to get a better idea of where memory consumption is occurring on the server and will allow you to find containers that need their resource usage corrected.

```
[root@gotham log]# vzmemcheck -v
Output values in %
CTID      LowMem LowMem     RAM MemSwap MemSwap   Alloc   Alloc   Alloc
          util   commit    util   util  commit    util    commit   limit
101        1.18 8868740482688.47   4.02    0.40 1169770694531.77    1.64 1169770694531.77 1199014961890702.25
-------------------------------------------------------------------------------
Summary:   1.18 8868740482688.47   4.02    0.40 1169770694531.77    1.64 1169770694531.77 1199014961890702.25
```

In the previous example, we used the `vzmemcheck` command with the `-v` flag to display the memory breakdown for each container.

vzmemcheck with the -A flag

It is also worth noting that you can use `vzmemcheck` with the -A flag either by itself or with the `-v` flag to display the memory values in MB.

```
vzmemcheck -A
```

The /var/log/vzctl.log file

The majority of the output from OpenVZ is going to be written to `/var/log/messages` and the action output for `vzctl` is going to be written to `/var/log/vzctl.log`.

Understanding the /var/log/vzctl.log file

The `vzctl.log` file is the logfile were `vzctl` stores the output for its actions. The logfile is rotated monthly for historical reference.

If you run the `ls /var/log/vzctl.*` command, you will get the following output:

```
ls /var/log/vzctl.*
/var/log/vzctl.log /var/log/vzctl.log-20120221
```

Here is a sample output of the current logfile:

```
less /var/log/vzctl.log
```

```
2012-11-30T02:30:32-0500 vzctl : CT 101 : Setting CPU limit: 0
2012-11-30T02:30:32-0500 vzctl : CT 101 : Setting CPU units: 2000
2012-11-30T02:30:32-0500 vzctl : CT 101 : WARNING: Settings were not saved and w
ill be reset to original values at the next start (use --save flag)
2012-11-30T02:30:32-0500 vzctl : CT 101 : Stopping container ...
2012-11-30T02:33:01-0500 vzeventd : Started
2012-11-30T02:33:01-0500 vzctl : Setting CPU units: 1000
2012-11-30T02:33:01-0500 vzctl : WARNING: Settings were not saved and will be re
set to original values at the next start (use --save flag)
2012-11-30T02:33:25-0500 vzctl : CT 101 : Starting container ...
2012-11-30T02:33:26-0500 vzctl : CT 101 : Container is mounted
2012-11-30T02:33:26-0500 vzctl : CT 101 : Adding IP address(es): 192.168.2.117
2012-11-30T02:33:26-0500 vzctl : CT 101 : Setting CPU limit: 4
2012-11-30T02:33:26-0500 vzctl : CT 101 : Setting CPU units: 1500
2012-11-30T02:33:26-0500 vzctl : CT 101 : Setting CPUs: 2
2012-11-30T02:33:26-0500 vzctl : CT 101 : Set hostname: Gotham
2012-11-30T02:33:26-0500 vzctl : CT 101 : Container start in progress...
(END)
```

In the previous example, you can see the output from the last time we used the vzctl command to make changes to the CPU limits of container 101. If you need to go and reference the changes that have been made using vzctl, use this log.

Summary

In this chapter, we discussed the various important files on the server that you are going to use as an administrator on a day-to-day basis. We also discussed CPU management on the server, where you learned how to set a guarantee for CPU time for a container and also how to allocate the amount of CPUs that are available for each container.

We then discussed how to use the vzmemcheck command to check the amount of memory that is currently being used by the server and also used the -v flag to check the amount of memory that is being used per container.

Finally, we discussed the different logfiles that can be used to find information about OpenVZ in /var/log/messages and information about the actions that have been made using vzctl in /var/log/vzctl.log.

In the next chapter, we will learn how to set up, configure, and administer containers using a web-based configuration program: OpenVZ Web Panel.

5
Using OpenVZ
Web Panel – Part One

In this chapter, we are going to discuss the web administration tool for OpenVZ, aptly called OpenVZ Web Panel. OpenVZ Web Panel allows you to administer your OpenVZ server from a web-based GUI instead of administering it from the command line. You can manage just about every aspect of OpenVZ from OpenVZ Web Panel.

In this chapter, you will learn:

- Installing OpenVZ Web Panel
- Configuring `/etc/owp.conf`
- Configuring `/opt/ovz-web-panel/config/config.yml`
- Logging in to OpenVZ Web Panel
- Downloading OS templates
- Creating a container
- Changing the settings for a container

OpenVZ Web Panel

OpenVZ Web Panel is a web-based GUI created by Alexei Yuzhakov that allows you to create and manage containers and hardware resources on your server.

Installing OpenVZ Web Panel

You can install OpenVZ Web Panel by running a `wget` command as the root user to download the software to your server as follows:

```
wget -O - http://ovz-web-panel.googlecode.com/svn/installer/ai.sh | sh
```

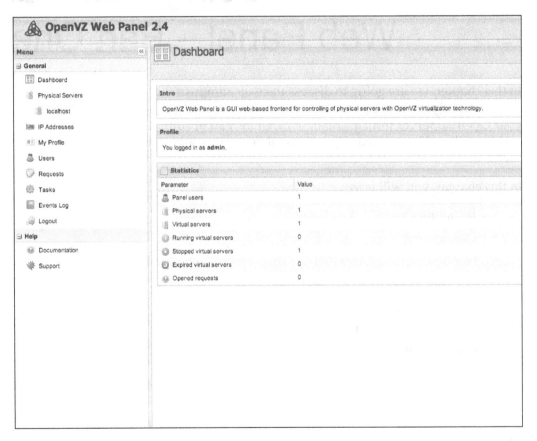

When the installation finishes, you will be notified that the install directory is /opt/ovz-web-panel and that it is currently starting services. Then, it gives you the IP address and port that you want to use in order to access OpenVZ from your web browser.

An example output is shown as follows:

Product was installed into: /opt/ovz-web-panel/

Starting services...

Starting OpenVZ Web Panel...

Starting watchdog daemon...

[OK] Watchdog daemon was started.

Starting web server webrick on 0.0.0.0:3000...

[OK] Web server was started.

Starting hardware node daemon...

[OK] Hardware node daemon was started.

Syncing hardware nodes states...

[OK] Hardware nodes information was synced.

Adding localhost to the list of controlled servers...

Panel should be available at:

http://localhost:3000

Default credentials: admin/admin

In the previous example, you will see the line **Starting web server webrick on 0.0.0.0:3000**. This line is okay and is what it should default to. This means that OpenVZ Web Panel is currently listening on any IP address that has been assigned to the server on port 3000. In the next section, we will learn how to change the IP address to a specific IP address and how to change the port number as well.

Configuring /etc/owp.conf

Once the installation is finished, you will want to make a few changes to the conf file for OpenVZ Web Panel. The conf file is located in /etc/owp.conf. In this section, we are going to go over the installation directory for OpenVZ Web Panel. Under this section, you will learn about /etc/owp.conf. This configuration file is the core file of the OpenVZ installation, as you can change how the program looks for certain files, what IP address OpenVZ listens to, what web server software is used, and also set up and provide SSL support.

- **Installation directory**: The installation directory is the directory where you have OpenVZ Web Panel installed. By default, it is currently installed to /opt/ovz-web-panel/. If you want to move the installation, you can move the files to the directory that you want (/usr/local/ovz-web-panel/), then update the option in the config file, and save your changes. It is not recommended to change this setting.

- **Web server software**: The default web server that OpenVZ Web Panel uses is WEBrick. WEBrick is a Ruby library that provides web services for both HTTP and HTTPS. If necessary, you can switch your web server to Mongrel instead of WEBrick.

- **Web server port**: The default port that OpenVZ web server is set to 3000. You can change the port to any open port that is currently available on your server.

- **Binding IP address**: The default IP address that OpenVZ web panel listens to is 0.0.0.0. What this means is that it will listen on all network interfaces. You can change this to any IP address that is currently available on your server.

- **SSL support**: The default setting for SSL is set to off. If you have a SSL certificate that you have installed on the server and you would like to access your site by using the HTTPS protocol instead of HTTP, you can set SSL to SSL =on. Please note that while OpenVZ Web Panel comes with a default SSL certificate, it's not meant to be used on a live site. If you have your own certificates, place them in /opt/ovz-web-panel/config/certs.

- **Web server lock file**: The web server lock file is the file that determines whether OpenVZ Web Panel is running or not. By default, the location is set to /var/local/owp. It is not recommended to change this location.

If you make any changes to the /etc/owp.conf file, you have to restart OpenVZ Web Panel. You can do this by running the following command:

1. **/etc/init.d/owp restart**

This will restart the web server and the OpenVZ services on the server.

Configuring /opt/ovz-web-panel/config/ config.yml

Another configuration file that you will make changes to from time to time is the `config.yml` file located at `/opt/ovz-web-panel/config`.

This configuration file allows you to make changes to the following:

- OS templates
- Branding
- Hardware daemon
- Help files
- Updates

When you open the config file in a file editor, you will see the following:

```
hw_daemon:
  port: 7767

os_templates:
  mirror:
    host: download.openvz.org
    path: /template/
ip_restriction:
  admin_ips: "192.168.0.1, 192.168.0.2"
```

Hardware daemon

The hardware daemon settings are configuration options for the hardware daemon. The default port is `7767`, which is used to communicate with hardware daemons on different servers.

You can also add a `timeout` option that is not currently listed by adding the `timeout` argument under `hw_daemon`. The `timeout` argument gives you the option to add a maximum timeout when trying to communicate with other hardware daemons.

- **OS Template**: The OS Template options allow you to add additional template mirrors to your OpenVZ Web Panel.
- **IP restrictions**: The IP restrictions options allow you to add restrictions to the IP addresses that are on your network.

- **Branding**: You can also add additional features to the `config.yml` file. One of them is an option to hide the version of **OpenVZ Web Panel** (**OWP**) that you are currently using. To set this option, you will want to add an option for branding named `branding` and add a suboption for show-version: `false`.

- **Help files**: You can add options for custom help files by adding a category for `help`, a subheading for each help file, and the URL you want it to point to.

```
Example:
help:
admin_doc_url: http:customesite.com/AdminGuide
user_doc_url: http://http://customesite.com /UserGuide
support_url: "http://customesite.com /Support"
```

- Updates: You can set an option to disable checks for update. With this option disabled, OpenVZ Web Panel will ignore any notifications of future updates. To disable updates, add a section for updates; the `disabled = true` setting disables checks for update.

LDAP

Instead of using basic login settings for OpenVZ Web Panel, you can configure it to use LDAP as your authentication method. To set this up, you have to add a section for LDAP and then add several settings under LDAP:

- `enabled: true`: This enables LDAP

- `host: "ldap.ldapserver.com"`: This tells the LDAP function which host to look for authentication

- `login_pattern: "uid=<login>,ou=people,dc=example,dc=com"`: This is the type of login pattern that is being used.

The following is an example:

```
ldap:
  enabled: true
  host: "ldap.ldapserver.com"
  login_pattern: "uid=<login>,ou=people,dc=example,dc=com"
```

If you make any changes to the `/opt/ovz-web-panel/config/config.yml` file, you need to restart OpenVZ Web Panel. You can do this by running the following command:

`/etc/init.d/owp restart`

This will restart the web server and the OpenVZ services on the server.

Logging in to OpenVZ Web Panel

To log in to OpenVZ Web Panel, you have to open your web browser and use the following URL:

```
http://<servers IP Address> 3000
```

In the previous example, you used the main IP address that you set for your server to access your installation of OpenVZ Web Panel. This address will vary depending on what you set your IP address to. The default login to access your panel is the username `admin` and the password `admin`. From the login screen, you can also choose the default language for your OpenVZ Web Panel installation as well, as shown in the following screenshot:

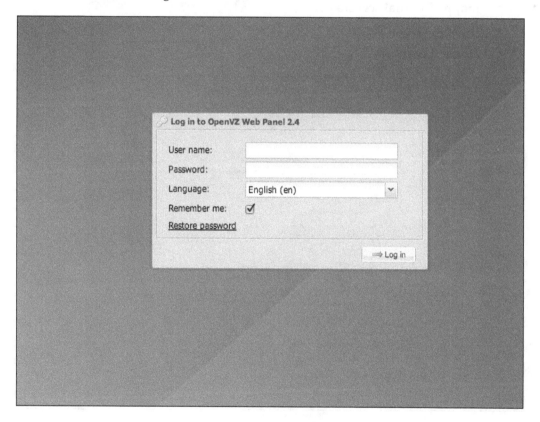

Dashboard

When you are logging in to OpenVZ Web Panel for the first time, your default page is the dashboard. The dashboard page gives you an overview of which user you are logged in as, and it shows you the following statistical information for total of each of the following listed on your server:

- **Panel users**
- **Physical servers**
- **Virtual servers**
- **Running virtual servers**
- **Stopped virtual servers**
- **Expired virtual servers**
- **Opened requests**

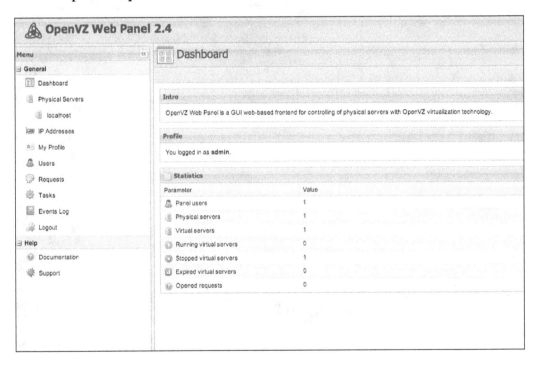

Physical servers

The physical server's page lists the actual servers that are connected to your OpenVZ Web Panel installation. By default, the first physical server you will see listed is localhost. You can connect more than one OpenVZ server to your OpenVZ installation to manage all of your servers from a single location instead of installing OpenVZ Web Panel on all of your servers that require multiple logins to manage.

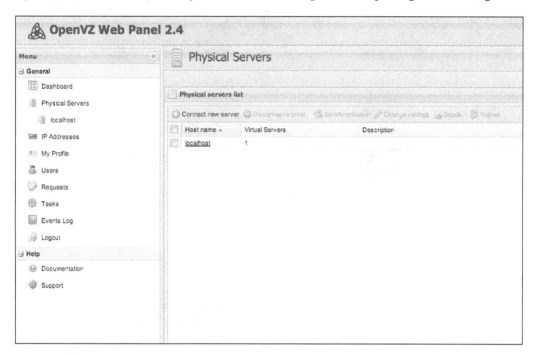

Localhost

Localhost is a subsection of physical servers; this is the first and primary physical server that is connected to OpenVZ Web Panel. At the top of this page, you have two buttons:

- **OS Templates**

- **Server Templates**

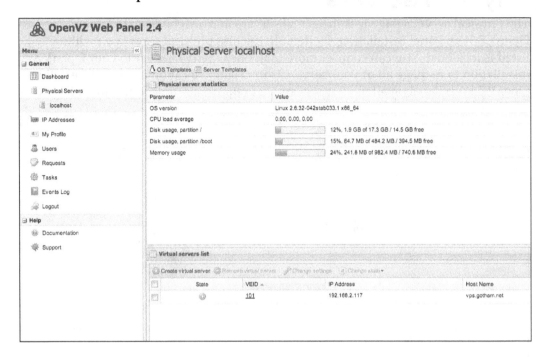

OS templates

The OS template page will provide you list of all of the OS templates that you currently have installed on your server. It also allows you to install a new OS template and remove any templates that have already been installed on the server.

Installing a new OS template

Clicking on the **Install New OS Template** button will bring up a menu with three tabs: **Official**, **Contributed**, and **URL**. The **Official** tab allows you to choose a template that has been officially released from OpenVZ.

The **Contributed** tab allows you to choose unofficial templates that have been added by other OpenVZ users, and the **URL** tab allows you to upload a customized template that you may have created yourself or found elsewhere on the Internet.

To add a template to your server, perform the following steps:

1. Click the **Official** tab.
2. Check the box for **centos6-x86_64**.
3. Click on the **Install** button.
4. You will see that an information box appears, stating that the OS template's installation was scheduled. The new template should appear after some time.
5. Click on **OK**.

This will add a template for the current CentOS distribution to your list of installed OS templates on your server.

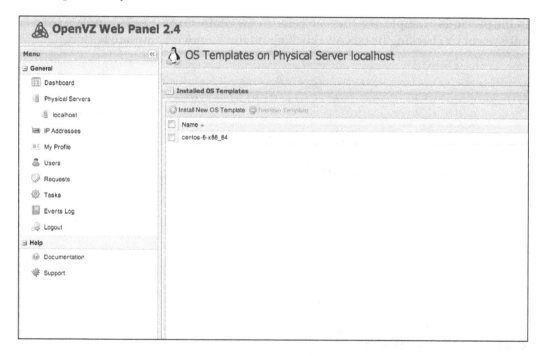

Removing a template

The **Remove Template** button allows you to select a template that you want to remove and delete it from the server.

To remove a template, perform the following steps:

1. Check the box for **centos6-x86_64**.

2. Click on the **Remove Template** button.

3. A confirmation box will appear, asking you to confirm that you want to remove the selected OS templates.

4. Click on **OK**.

In the previous example, we chose to remove the **centos6-x86_64** OS template from our system by checking its box and clicking on the **Remove Template** button.

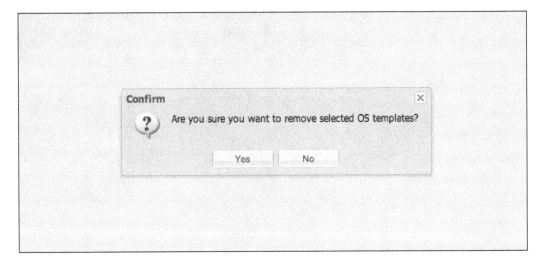

Server templates

Server templates are resource templates for your containers. They set default limits for the resources your container is allowed to use, including disk space, memory, swap, CPU limits, number of CPUs, and CPU limit percentage. You can also set the default DNS server as well as options to boot the container on start.

Templates are ideal to configure for your server, as they will save you time when you create your container by allowing you to preconfigure the container settings instead of having to set them manually every time.

The following server templates come preconfigured:

- **basic**
- **light**
- **unlimited**
- **vswap-1024m**
- **vswap-512m**
- **vswap-254m**

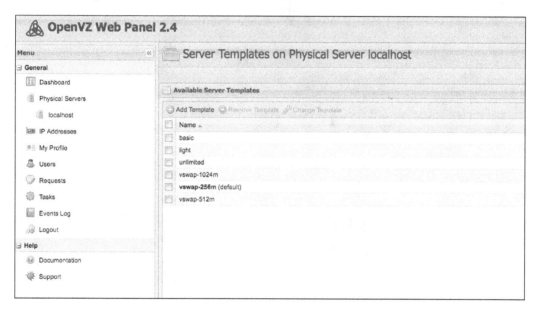

Adding a server template

Besides the preconfigured templates, you can also create your own templates by clicking on the **Add Template** button. You can give your container a name, set the amount of disk space you want your container to use, and set the amount of memory that you want the container to use. You can also configure your CPU units, numbers of CPUs, and CPU limit (if needed) and also choose if you want to start the container on boot. When you finish configuring your settings, you can click on the **Create** button to add your custom server template.

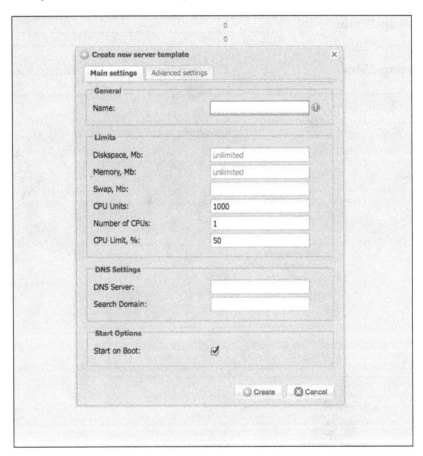

To add a server template to your server, perform the following steps:

1.   Click on the **Add Template** button.

2.   Type a name in the **Name** textbox, Star.

3.   Type the amount of disk space you want to use for your container in the **Diskspace** textbox, 2000.

4. Type the amount of memory that you want to use for your container in the **Memory** textbox, 256.

5. Type the amount of swap you want to use for your container in the **Swap** textbox (normally double the amount of RAM you have installed), 256.

6. Check the box for **Start on Boot**.

7. Click on the **Create** button.

8. You will see an information box appear, stating that the OS templates installation was scheduled and the new template should appear after some time.

9. Click on **OK**.

This will add a server template to your list of installed servers' templates on your server. If you want to follow along with the settings that I have added for the container template that we have created, these are shown in the following screenshot:

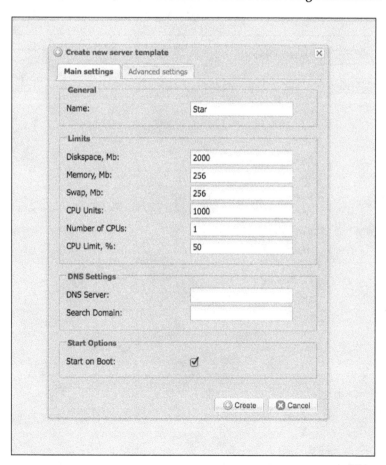

Changing a server template

You can change the current settings that you have for any of the server templates that you have installed on your server. To change a template, place a check mark in the box for the template you wish to update and click on the **Change Template** button. To change a template, perform the following steps:

1. Check the box of the template that you want to change. In this example, I selected the star template that was just created.

2. Click on the **Change Template** button.

3. Change the **Diskspace, Mb** value for the star template from 2000 to 4000.

4. Click on the **Save** button.

5. In the previous example, we selected the star server template and changed the value of the containers total disk space from 2000 MB to 4000 MB. Then, click on the **Save** button to confirm our changes.

Removing a server template

The **Remove Template** button allows you to select a template that you want to remove and delete it from the server.

To remove a template, perform the following steps:

1. Check the box for **star**.

2. Click on the **Remove Template** button.

3. A confirmation box will appear, asking you to confirm that you want to remove the selected server template.

4. Click on **OK**.

In the previous example, we chose to remove the server template named **star** from our system by checking its box and clicking on the **Remove Template** button.

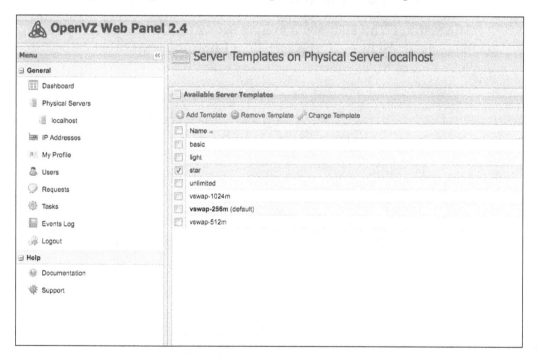

Virtual servers list

In the second half of the **localhost** page, all the virtual server containers that are created on your server are listed. From this part of the page, you are able to do the following:

- Create a virtual server

- Remove a virtual server

- Change the settings

- Change the state

Managing the virtual server

Clicking on the **Create virtual server** button will bring up a menu with two tabs: **Main Settings** and **Additional Settings**.

- **Main Settings**: This allows you to enter **Server ID, OS Template, Server Template, IP Address, Host Name, Root Password**, and **Owner** of the container you are creating.

- **Additional Settings**: This tab allows you to set limits for your container. The limits you can set are: **Disk Space**, **Memory**, **Swap**, **CPU Units**, **Number of CPUs**, **CPU Limit**, **Expiration date** of the container, **DNS Server**, and whether or not you want to start the container on boot and/or after creation. Then, an option is defined for daily backup of the container.

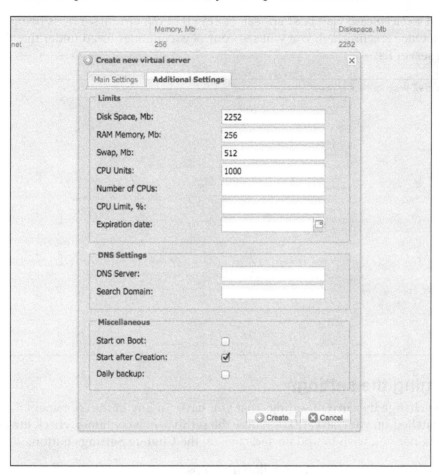

Making a virtual server

To make a new virtual server, perform the following steps:

1. Click on the **Create virtual server** button.

2. Type a **Server ID**, 102.

3. Choose a **OS Template**, centos-6-x86_64.

4. Choose a **Server Template**, vswap-256m.

5. Type an **IP address**, `192.167.2.117`.

6. Type a **Host Name**, `Star`.

7. Type a **Root Password**.

8. Click on the **Create** button.

You will see a "please wait box" appear, stating that the virtual server is being created. Once it is finished, you will see your new container listed under the virtual server list.

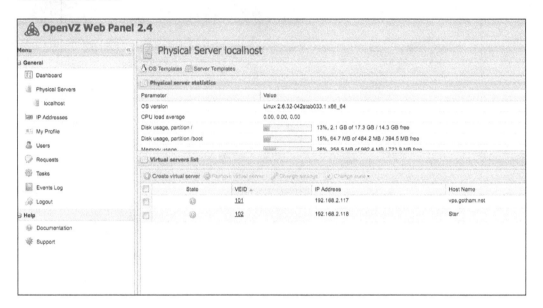

Changing the settings

You can change the current settings that you have for any of the containers that you have installed on your server. To change the settings of a container, check the box for the container you wish to update and click on the **Change Settings** button.

To change a setting, perform the following steps:

1. Check the box of the container that you want to change. In this example, I selected container **102** that was just created.

2. Click on the **Settings** button.

3. Under description, add `Test Container 1`.

4. Click on the **Save** button.

5. In the previous example, we selected and used the container we just made (102) and changed the value of the containers description to **Test Container 1**. Now, click on the **Save** button to confirm our changes.

Removing a virtual server

The **Remove Virtual Server** button allows you to select a container that you want to remove and delete it from the server.

To remove a container, perform the following steps:

1. Check the box for the container **102**.

2. Click on the **Remove virtual server** button.

3. A confirmation box will appear, asking you to confirm that you want to remove the selected server template.

4. Click on **OK**.

5. In the previous example, we chose to remove the container **102** from our system by checking its box and clicking on the **Remove virtual server** button.

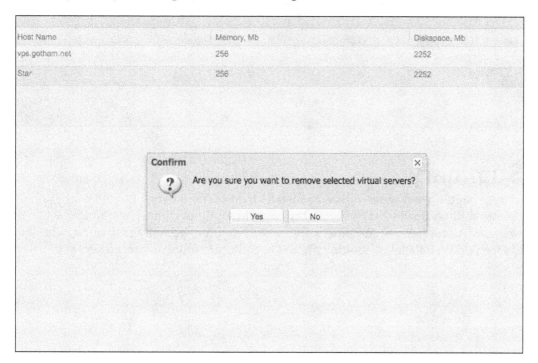

Changing the state of the container

The **Change state** button allows you to change the state of your container to several different options: **Start**, **Stop**, and **Restart**. They are explained as follows:

- **Start**: This allows you to start the container if the container is stopped
- **Stop**: This allows you to stop the container if the container is started
- **Restart**: This allows you to restart the container if the container is started

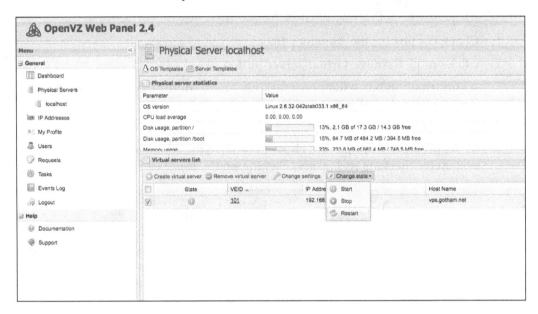

Summary

In this chapter, we discussed how to install OpenVZ Web Panel; how to configure custom settings inside /etc/ow.config; how to set up OS templates; and how to create, edit, and remove containers. In the next chapter, we will finish our discussion of OpenVZ Web Panel by looking at how to configure more advanced settings.

6
Using OpenVZ
Web Panel – Part Two

In *Chapter 5*, *Using OpenVZ Web Panel – Part One*, we discussed how to install OpenVZ Web Panel and also how to add OS templates and create containers. In this chapter on OpenVZ Web Panel, you will learn how to use the OpenVZ Web Panel GUI to do the following:

- Understand the virtual server information page
- Reinstall containers
- Back up containers
- Configure network settings
- Review event logs
- Manage tasks
- Manage requests
- Manage OpenVZ Web Panel accounts

Understanding the virtual server information page

The virtual server information page contains the resources that you need to manage your containers on the server. Clicking on the container ID on the virtual servers list will take you to the virtual server information page that has the following options:

- **Change state**
- **Change settings**
- **Limits**
- **Tools**

These options can be seen in the following screenshot:

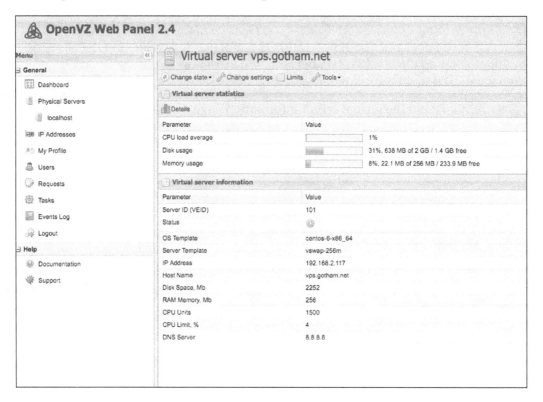

Change state

The **Change state** options on the virtual server page are the same as the ones that we presented in *Chapter 5, Using OpenVZ Web Panel – Part One*. You have the following options **Change state**:

- **Start**: Choosing this option allows you to start the container if it has stopped
- **Stop**: Choosing this option allows you to stop the container if it has started
- **Restart**: Choosing this option allows you to restart the container if it has already started

Change settings

You can change the current settings for any of the containers that you have installed on your server. To change the settings of a container, place a check mark in the box for the container you wish to update and click on the **Change settings** button. To change the settings, you can do the following:

1. Click on the **Settings** button.
2. Under **Description**, add: `Web Development Test Server`.
3. Click on the **Save** button.

Limits

The **Limits** button will open an option page that allows you to view and change the containers limits as needed. Please note that if you change the limits without fully understanding the results, it could cause stability issues with your container.

To change the limits on the page, you can do the following:

1. Click on the **Limits** button.
2. Double-click on the **Barrier** field for **NUMPROC**.
3. Change the value from **unlimited** to `200`.
4. Double-click on the **Limit** field for **NUMPROC**.
5. Change the value from **unlimited** to `600`.
6. Click on **Save.**

In the preceding example, we clicked on the **Limits** button for the container 101 and changed the values for the **Barrier** and **Limit** fields of **NUMPROC** from **unlimited** to 200/600 so that our container has a limit on the number of processes that it is allowed to open at one time.

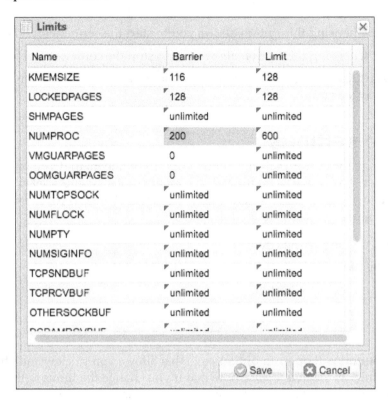

Tools

The **Tools** option gives you several actions that you can choose from to take on the container. You can choose from the following options:

- **Reinstall**
- **Backup**
- **Clone**
- **Create Template**
- **Console**

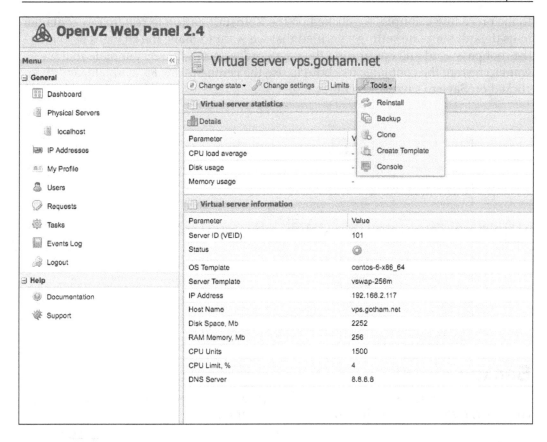

Reinstall

Clicking on the **Reinstall** button will destroy the container and then recreate your container with its default template settings.

[This will delete all the data and programs from your container.]

To reinstall your container to its default settings, perform the following steps:

1. Click on **Reinstall** (this will open the **Reinstall** menu).
2. Type your root password.
3. Confirm your root password.
4. Choose the **centos-6-x86_64** template.
5. Click on **Save**.

In the preceding example, we clicked on the **Reinstall** button to restore our container to its default template settings, verified that we want to make the changes by typing the root password and confirming the password, selected the OS template that we want to restore the container to, chose to use the **centos-6-x86_64** template, and then clicked on **Save** to save our changes.

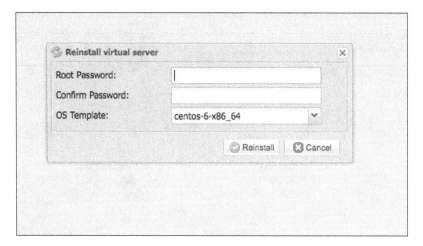

Backup

The **Backup** button takes you to the backup page that allows you to back up the container, restore the container from a backup, or delete a saved backup.

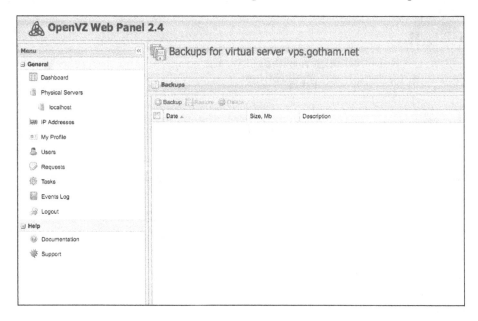

Backing up a container

To back up a container, you will want to click on the **Backup** button. Once you click on the **Backup** button, a menu will appear asking you to type a description of your backup and also prompts you to choose a server state while you perform your backup. You can suspend, stop, or choose to keep your server running during the backup. The recommended option is to suspend your server.

To back up your container, you will want to do the following:

1. Click on **Backup**.
2. Type a description for the backup: `Container 101 Backup`.
3. Choose **Server state** as **suspend**.
4. Click on **Create**.

When you click on the **Create** button, a pop-up box will appear to let you know that your backup has started and will take some time to complete.

In the preceding example, we chose to create a backup for the container 101 by clicking on the **Backup** button. Then, we created a description for our backup named `Container 101 Backup` and also chose to suspend the server during the backup. Finally, we clicked on the **Create** button to start our backup.

When the backup is complete, you will see it listed in the backup screen. It will provide you with the date, size, and description of the backup.

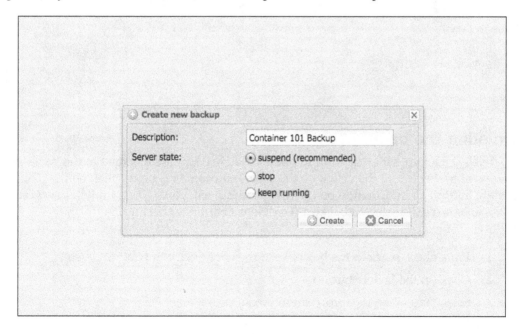

Restoring the container

To restore the container from a backup, you will have to select the backup you want to restore by putting a check mark in the box next to the backup and clicking on the **Restore** button. When you click on the **Restore** button, a menu will appear asking you if you are sure you want to restore the selected backup and inform you that the server will not be available during the restore.

To perform a container restore, perform the following steps:

1. Check the box next to the backup you want to restore.
2. Click on **Restore**.
3. Select **Yes** when the information box appears.

When you select **Yes** to continue with your restore, another information box will appear to tell you that the restore procedure has started and will take some time to finish. Click on the **Ok** button to continue.

In the preceding example, we selected the container 101 to be restored by checking the box next to the container name and clicking on the **Restore** button. When the information box appeared, we acknowledged that we wanted to continue with the restore.

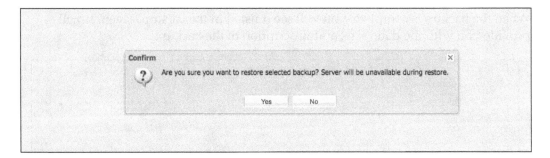

Deleting the backup

To delete a backup, you will want to put a check mark in the box next to the backup you want to delete and then click on the **Delete** button. When you click on the **Delete** button, an information box will appear and ask you to confirm whether you want to remove the selected backup. To delete a container backup, perform the following steps:

1. Put a check mark in the box next to the container you want to delete.
2. Click on the **Delete** button.
3. Select **Yes** when the information box appears.

In the preceding example, we selected the backup for the container 101 to be deleted by putting a check mark in the box next to the backup and clicking on the **Delete** button. When the information box appeared asking us to confirm the deletion, we clicked on the **Yes** button.

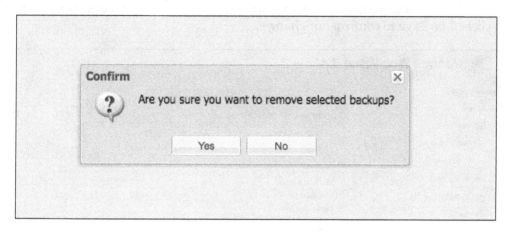

Clone

Cloning your container allows you to create an exact image of your container, which you can use to quickly create another container. To clone your container, you will want to select a clone from the **Tools** drop-down menu. When you select a clone, a menu will appear that allows you to type the server or container ID, root password, IP address, and host name of the new container.

To clone a container, perform the following steps:

1. Select **Clone** from the **Tools** menu.
2. Type the **Server ID**: 102.
3. Type the **Root Password**: pass12345.
4. Confirm the **Root Password**: pass12345.
5. Type the **IP address**: 192.168.2.118.
6. Type the **Host Name**: metropolis.yourserver.com.
7. Click on **Save**.

In the preceding example, we created a clone of the container 101 by clicking on the **Clone** button in the **Tools** menu. When the menu appeared, we set the container ID as 102, root password as pass12345, IP address as 192.168.2.118 (note that the IP address will vary depending on your network setup), and then the hostname as metropolis.yourdomain.com, where your domain is your custom domain, and then we clicked on **Save** to confirm our changes.

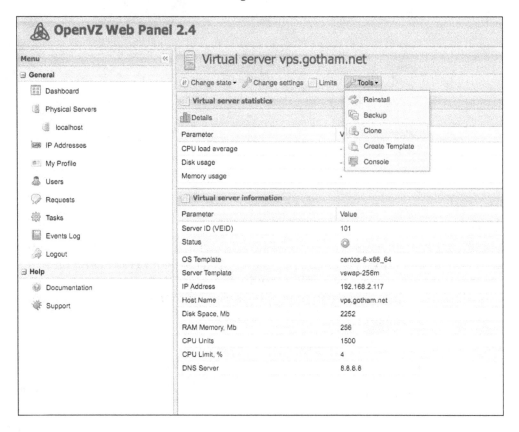

Create Template

You can create an OS template, which you can use when creating future containers by clicking on the **Create Template** button in the **Tools** drop-down menu. When you click on **Create Template**, a menu will appear asking you to name your new template.

To create a new template, perform the following steps:

1. Select **Create Template** from the **Tools** menu.
2. Type **Name** as centos-6-x86_64-container101.
3. Click on **Create**.

In the preceding example, we created an OS template based on the container 101 by clicking on the **Create Template** button from the **Tools** drop-down menu, choosing the name `centos-6-x86-container101`, and then clicking on the **Create** button.

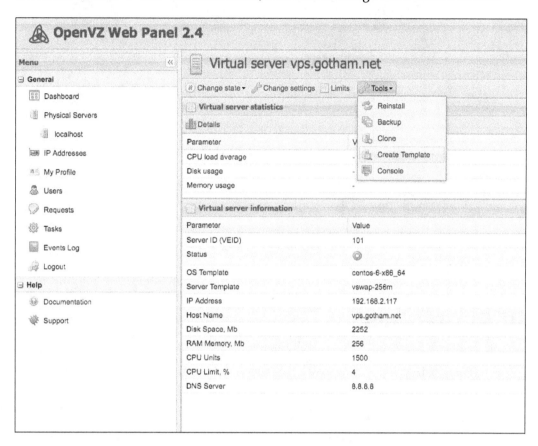

Console

Console allows you to run commands on your container directly from OpenVZ Web; Console is a great option if you want to quickly view extended stats on the container or perform any quick edit to OpenVZ via the command line without needing to open an ssh session.

To use **Console** to run `df -h` in order to view the partition sizes on the container, you will want to do the following:

1. Select **Console** from the **Tools** menu.
2. Type `df -h`.
3. Click on **Run**.

In the preceding example, we chose **Console** from the **Tools** menu and sent the `df -h` command to the container to examine the size of the container's partitions.

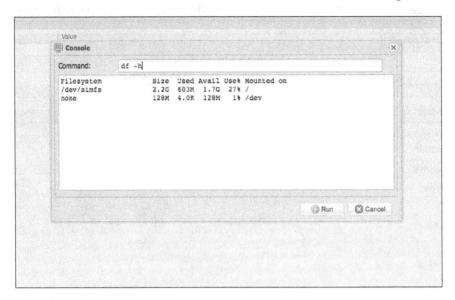

IP Addresses

The **IP Addresses** screen has the following two sections:

- **IP pools list**
- **IP addresses list**

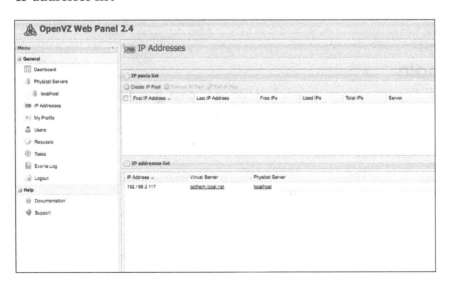

IP pools list

The **IP pools list** section allows you to create, remove, or edit IP pools that you can dedicate to your VPS node. This will allow you to manage the IP addresses that are on your node very easily.

Create IP pool

Clicking on the **Create IP pool** button will bring up a menu that allows you to choose a range of IP addresses dedicated to your server. This allows you to choose from the available IP addresses when you create a container on your server.

To create an IP pool on your node, you can do the following:

1. Click on the **Create IP pool** button.
2. Type the first IP address that you want to use in your IP range: `192.168.2.117`.
3. Type the second IP address that you want to use in your IP range: `192.168.2.121`.
4. Choose your `localhost` server.
5. Click on the **Create** button.

In the preceding example, we created an IP pool by clicking on the **Create IP pool** button. We then chose IP addresses for **First IP address** and **Second IP address** in the range. For example, I used the range `192.168.2.117-192.168.2.121`. The choice of IP addresses will depend on your network setup. We then chose a server (`localhost`) to apply the range to and clicked on the **Create** button to finish creating the range.

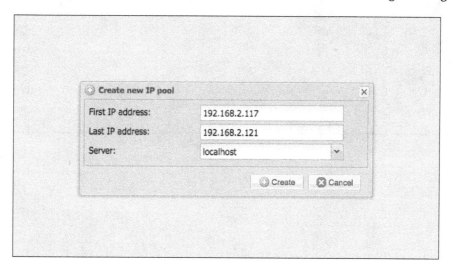

Edit IP pool

The **Edit IP pool** button allows you to select an IP range that you have previously created and add or remove IPs from the range.

To add additional IP addresses to the range, perform the following steps:

1. Check the current IP range's box.
2. Click on the **Edit IP pool** button.
3. Edit the second IP address: `192.168.2.125`.
4. Click on the **Save** button.

In the preceding example, we edited the previously created IP address range, which was `192.168.2.117-192.168.2.121` to include four more IP addresses making the new range `192.168.2.117-192.168.2.125` and then clicked on the **Save** button to save our changes.

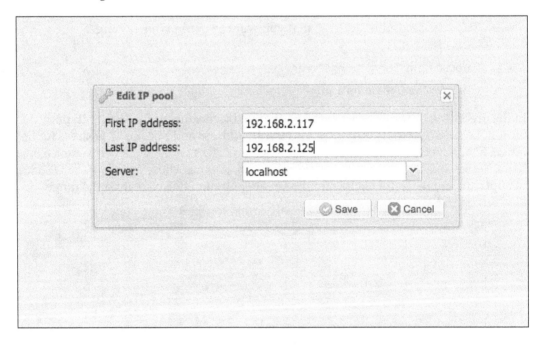

Remove IP pool

The **Remove IP pool** button allows you to select an IP range that was previously created and remove it from the server.

To remove an IP range, perform the following steps:

1. Check the IP range box that you want to remove.
2. Click on the **Remove IP pool** button.
3. Click on the **Yes** button when the confirmation box appears and asks you whether you are sure about removing the selected IP pools.

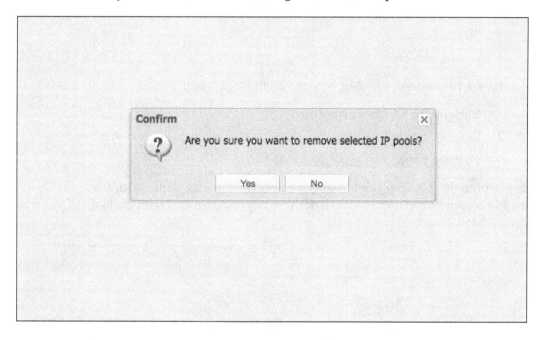

In the preceding example, we removed the IP pool that we previously created by selecting the IP pool, clicking on the **Remove IP pool** button, and then acknowledging that we really want to remove the pool by clicking on the **Yes** button.

IP addresses list

The IP addresses list will display all the current IP addresses that are being used on the server. As more containers are created and more IP addresses are used, more containers will appear in this list.

My Profile

The **My Profile** section will allow you to update settings regarding your OpenVZ Web Panel account. You can change the following:

- Your current password
- Contact name
- E-mail address

To change your e-mail address, you can do the following:

1. Click on the **My Profile** button.
2. Enter your new e-mail address, admin@yourdomain.com, in the **E-mail** field.
3. Click on **Save**.

In the preceding example, we changed the current e-mail address for the **admin** account to an admin e-mail address of your own and then clicked on the **Save** button.

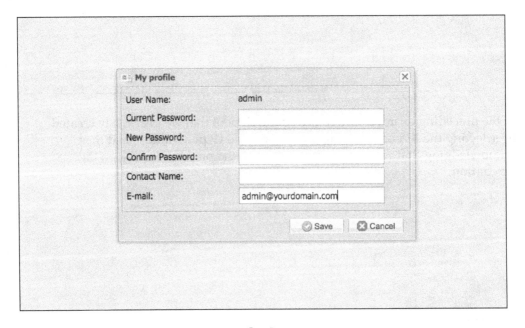

Users

The **Users** section allows you to manage user roles on your server. Besides the main admin account, you may create a user account for each of the containers. You can choose the following options:

- **Add User**
- **Delete User**
- **Edit User**

Add User

The **Add User** button allows you to add a user to your server. You may need to add a user account to a container where the owner of the container can log in and make changes.

To add a user to a container, perform the following steps:

1. Click on the **Add User** button.
2. Enter `mfurman` as the login name for the user.
3. Enter `pass12345` as the password for the user.
4. Confirm that the password for the user is `pass12345`.
5. Enter `Mark Furman` as the contact name.
6. Enter `mark@markfurman.net` as the user's e-mail address.
7. Choose **Admin/Virtual Server Owner: Virtual Server Owner** as the role for the user.
8. Click on the **Create** button.

In the preceding example, we clicked on the **Add User** button to add a user to the server with the following information:

- **Login Name**: `mfurman`
- **Password**: `pass12345`
- **Contact Name**: `Mark Furman`
- **E-mail**: `mark@markfurman.net`
- **Role**: `Virtual Server Owner`

Then, we clicked on **Create** to finish creating the account.

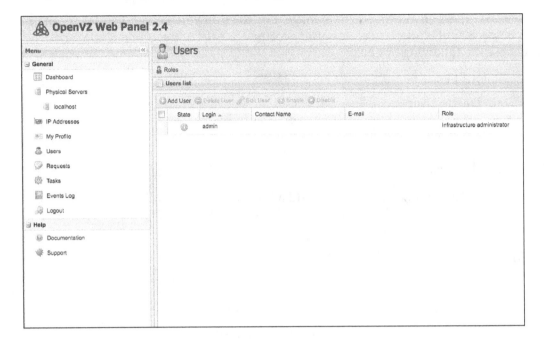

Edit User

The **Edit User** button allows you to change settings for the users that are currently created on your server. Under the **Edit User** section, you can change the following fields:

- Password
- Contact Name
- E-mail
- Role

To update the password for the user you just created, perform the following steps:

1. Check the user's box **mfurman**.
2. Click on the **Edit User** button.
3. Enter the new password abc123 in the **Password** field.
4. Enter abc123 in the **Confirm Password** field to confirm your password.
5. Click on the **Save** button.

In the preceding example, we selected the user (**mfurman**) that we wanted to update the password for by checking the box next to the user's name and then clicking on the **Edit User** button.

When the **Edit User** menu appears on the screen, we typed the new password (abc123) in the **Password** and **Confirm Password** fields and then clicked on the **Save** button to confirm our changes.

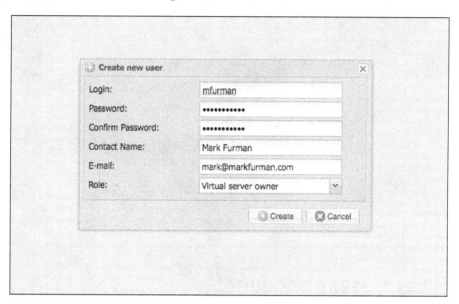

Enable/disable user account

You can select the **Enable User** or **Disable User** buttons to enable or disable a user account on the server, respectively.

Disabling a user's account

To disable a user, perform the following steps:

1. Check the **mfurman** user's box you want to disable.
2. Click on the **Disable** button.

In the preceding example, you checked the user's box that you wanted to disable (**mfurman**) and then clicked on the **Disable** button to disable the account. When the account is disabled, the status icon of the user will change from green to red to show that the account is now disabled.

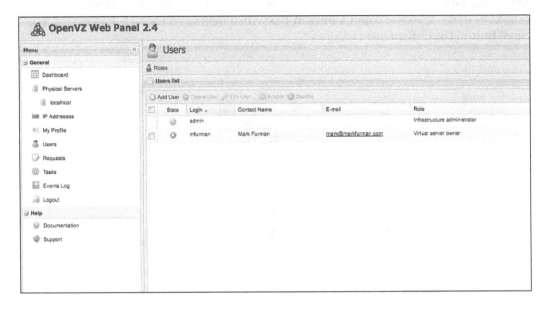

Enabling a user's account

To enable a user, perform the following steps:

1. Check the **mfurman** users box you want to enable.
2. Click on the **Enable** button.

In the preceding example, you checked the user's box that you wanted to enable (**mfurman**) and then clicked on the **Enable** button to enable the account. When the account is enabled, the status icon of the user will change from red to green to show that the account is now enabled.

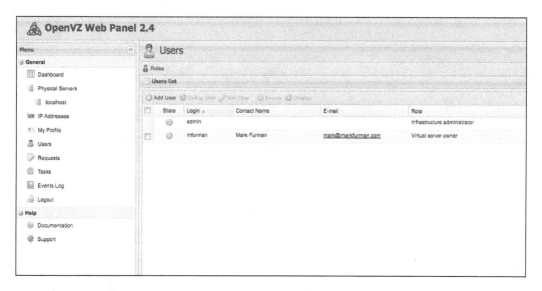

Delete User

The **Delete User** button allows you to remove a user account from the server. When a container is removed from the server, you will also want to remove the user associated with that container from the server as well.

To delete a user from the server, perform the following steps:

1. Check the **mfurman** users box that you want to delete.
2. Click on the **Delete User** button.
3. When the confirmation box appears, click on the **Yes** button.

In the preceding example, you deleted a user from the server by selecting the user and clicking on the **Delete User** button. Then, when the confirmation box appeared, you clicked on the **Yes** button to confirm that you wanted to remove the user.

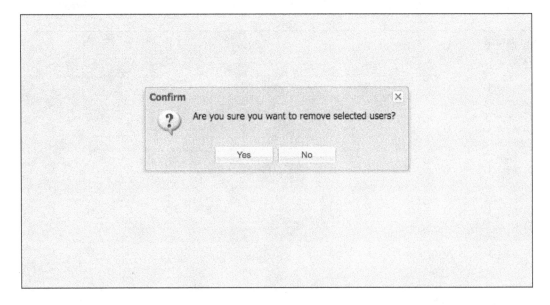

Requests

The **Requests** section allows you to create a support request. This is useful for users on the server that face issues with their container. They can create a request to the administrator of the server, and then the administrator can investigate the issue and update the status of the request.

The request screen allows you to choose the following options:

- **Create Request**
- **Delete Request**
- **Details**

Create Request

You can create a request to track an issue on the server or have the issue documented and resolved.

To create a request on the server, perform the following steps:

1. Click on the **Create Request** button.
2. Enter the subject of your request as `Please look into the RAM usage on my container`.
3. Enter the message of your request as `My container is running out of memory periodically, could you please look into this for me?`.
4. Click on the **Create** button.

In the preceding example, you created a request to have the RAM on your container looked at due to the container facing memory issues. You made the request by clicking on the **Create Request** button and adding the subject line `Please look into the RAM usage on my container` and the message of the request as `My container is running out of memory periodically, could you please look into this for me?`. Then, you clicked on the **Create** button to create the request.

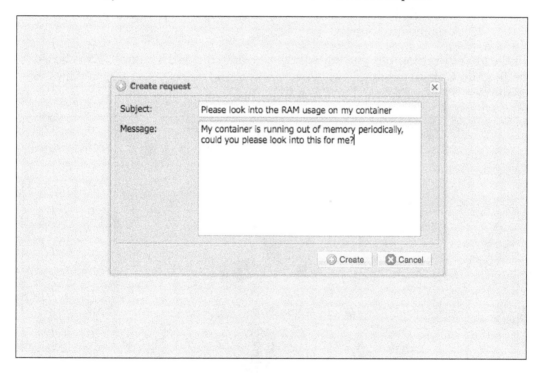

Details

You can look at the details of a request by clicking on the **Details** button; this will take you to the **Requests** page where you can choose the following options:

- **Add Comment**
- **Close Request**

Add comment

You can add a comment by clicking on the **Add Comment** button. Adding a comment will allow you to communicate with the user who created the request.

To add a comment to the request, you can do the following:

1. Click on the **Add Comment** button.
2. Enter a message, `Looking into your request`.
3. Click on the **Add** button.

In the preceding example, you added a comment to the user's request. You clicked on the **Add Comment** button and typed the `Looking into your request` message to the user. Then, you clicked on the **Add** button to save the comment.

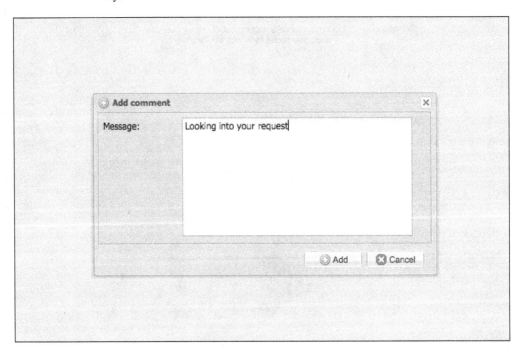

Close request

You can also close a request by clicking on the **Close Request** button to let the user who created the request know that the issue is now resolved.

To close a request on the server, you can click on the **Close Request** button.

In the preceding example, you closed the request from the user who wanted you to look into the issue with his/her RAM by clicking on the **Close Request** button. When you click on the **Close Request** button, it will take you back to the main request screen and change the state of the request to a green check mark to denote that the request has been completed.

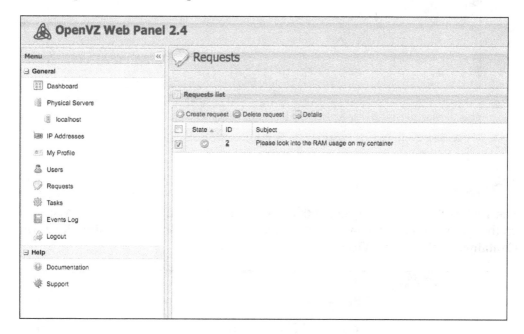

Delete Request

You can delete a request from the server by clicking on the **Delete Request** button. Deleting a request will allow you to manage the number of closed requests that are listed to keep the **Requests** screen clean.

To delete a request from the server, perform the following steps:

1. Check the box of the request that you would like to delete.
2. A confirmation box will appear asking you if you want to remove the request from the server. Click on the **Yes** button.

In the preceding example, you deleted the user's request from the server to clear the request screen. You did this by selecting the request that you want to delete, clicking on the box next to the request, and then clicking on the **Delete request** button.

A confirmation button appeared and asked you to confirm that you wanted to delete the request from the server and you clicked on the **Yes** button to confirm the deletion.

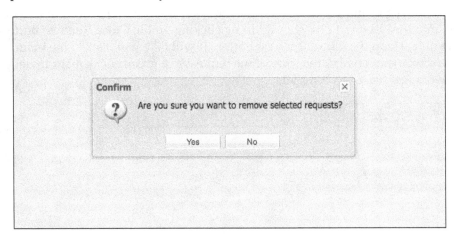

Tasks

The **Task** section shows any event that takes a significant amount of time to complete on the server. Some of the tasks that are listed in the section are **Container Restores**, **Container Backups**, and **OS template Installations**.

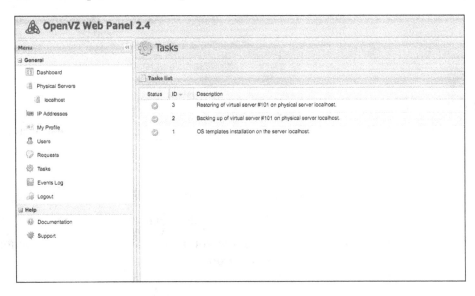

Events Log

The events log shows every other event that occurs on the server. This log can be viewed as an audit log, which can be used to see what a specific user has to do to a container in the event of an issue. Some examples of events are **Removing Requests**, **Request Comment creation**, **Users Created**, **Users Removed**, **Users Updated**, **Containers Created**, and **Containers Removed**.

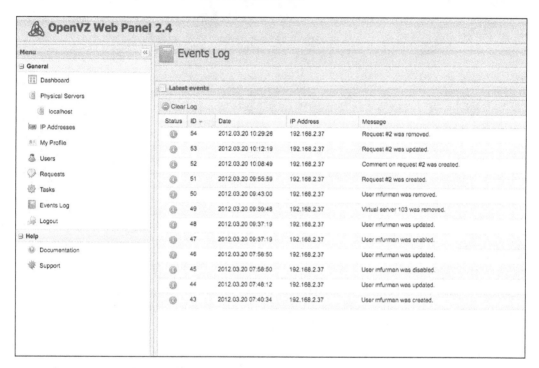

Logout

The logout section will allow you to log out of your OpenVZ Web Panel account.

To log out of OpenVZ Web Panel, you can do the following:

1. Click on the **Logout** button.
2. A confirmation box will appear asking you if you want to logout.
3. Click on **Yes** to confirm.

In the preceding example, you logged out of your OpenVZ Web Panel account by clicking on the **Logout** button and then clicking on the **Yes** button when the confirmation box appeared on the screen.

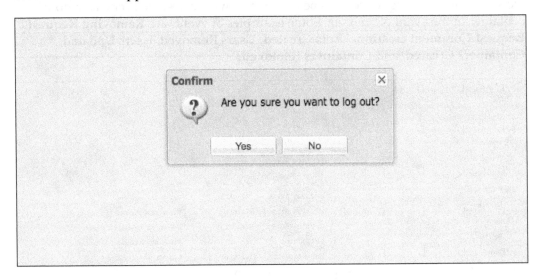

Summary

In this chapter, we went over the entire process of using OpenVZ Web Panel to install and administer our OpenVZ node. We went through the system requirements that are needed, how to install OpenVZ Web Panel on the server and how to create and remove OS templates and server templates.

We also went over how to create, edit, and remove VPS containers from the server, how to add, edit, and remove IP address pools from the server, how to add, edit, and remove users from the server, and how to create, update, and delete requests from the server. Finally, we went over the **Tasks** and **Events Log** sections.

Index

Thank you for buying
OpenVZ Essentials

About Packt Publishing

Packt, pronounced 'packed', published its first book "*Mastering phpMyAdmin for Effective MySQL Management*" in April 2004 and subsequently continued to specialize in publishing highly focused books on specific technologies and solutions.

Our books and publications share the experiences of your fellow IT professionals in adapting and customizing today's systems, applications, and frameworks. Our solution based books give you the knowledge and power to customize the software and technologies you're using to get the job done. Packt books are more specific and less general than the IT books you have seen in the past. Our unique business model allows us to bring you more focused information, giving you more of what you need to know, and less of what you don't.

Packt is a modern, yet unique publishing company, which focuses on producing quality, cutting-edge books for communities of developers, administrators, and newbies alike. For more information, please visit our website: www.packtpub.com.

About Packt Open Source

In 2010, Packt launched two new brands, Packt Open Source and Packt Enterprise, in order to continue its focus on specialization. This book is part of the Packt Open Source brand, home to books published on software built around Open Source licenses, and offering information to anybody from advanced developers to budding web designers. The Open Source brand also runs Packt's Open Source Royalty Scheme, by which Packt gives a royalty to each Open Source project about whose software a book is sold.

Writing for Packt

We welcome all inquiries from people who are interested in authoring. Book proposals should be sent to author@packtpub.com. If your book idea is still at an early stage and you would like to discuss it first before writing a formal book proposal, contact us; one of our commissioning editors will get in touch with you.

We're not just looking for published authors; if you have strong technical skills but no writing experience, our experienced editors can help you develop a writing career, or simply get some additional reward for your expertise.

CentOS 6 Linux Server Cookbook

ISBN: 978-1-84951-902-1   Paperback: 374 pages

A practical guide to installing, configuring, and administering the CentOS community-based enterprise server

1. Delivering comprehensive insight into CentOS server with a series of starting points that show you how to build, configure, maintain, and deploy the latest edition of one of the world's most popular community based enterprise servers.

2. Providing beginners and more experienced individuals alike with the opportunity to enhance their knowledge by delivering instant access to a library of recipes that addresses all aspects of CentOS server and put you in control.

Instant Nginx Starter

ISBN: 978-1-78216-512-5   Paperback: 48 pages

Implement the nifty features of nginx with this focused guide

1. Learn something new in an Instant! A short, fast, focused guide delivering immediate results.

2. Understand Nginx and its relevance to the modern web.

3. Install Nginx and explore the different methods of installation.

4. Configure and customize Nginx.

Please check **www.PacktPub.com** for information on our titles

Puppet 3 Cookbook

ISBN: 978-1-78216-976-5   Paperback: 274 pages

Build reliable, scalable, secure, and high-performance
systems to fully utilize the power of cloud computing

1. Use Puppet 3 to take control of your
    servers and desktops, with detailed
    step-by-step instructions.

2. Covers all the popular tools and frameworks
    used with Puppet: Dashboard, Foreman,
    and more.

3. Teaches you how to extend Puppet with
    custom functions, types, and providers.

4. Packed with tips and inspiring ideas for
    using Puppet to automate server builds,
    deployments, and workflows.

Packet Tracer Network Simulator

ISBN: 978-1-78217-042-6   Paperback: 134 pages

Simulate an unlimited number of devices on
a network using Packet Tracer

1. Configure Cisco devices using
    practical examples.

2. Simulate networking with multiple
    branch offices.

3. Create practical networking assessments.

Please check **www.PacktPub.com** for information on our titles